WELCOME TO OUR LIBERATION

YEARS
50

LEGAL

SIMON NAPIER-BELL

This edition © Red Planet Books Ltd 2019
Text © Simon Napier-Bell 2017-2019

ISBN: 978 1 9113 4620 3
Printed in the UK

Cover: Harry Gregory
Publisher: Mark Neeter

A donation from the sale of this book will be made to
The Terence Higgins Trust and The Albert Kennedy Trust

Red Planet Books
Tremough Innovation Centre,
Penryn, Cornwall TR10 9TA

www.redplanetzone.com

Email: info@redplanetzone.com

WELCOME TO OUR LIBERATION

YEARS

50

LEGAL

CONTENTS

FOREWORD

The idea came to me in 2017, the fiftieth anniversary of the decriminalisation of male homosexuality, that I would make a film to celebrate the occasion. But when I began to work on the interviews for it I realised it would have to be a book as well. There was too much of importance being said; too much that had real social relevance. In the end there were 50 hours of interviews, and the film could only incorporate 50 minutes of them.

A few people have asked me why there are so few women interviewees. The answer is, this was not a project about what it was like to be a homosexual. It was a project about what it was like to find you'd been born a criminal – that through no fault of your own you were in danger of committing a crime simply by living your life as a normal person. For men, homosexuality was illegal. For women it was not.

As with all creative works, I suppose it was also the story of the author – me. And as such it was created very much from my own point of view, which was that of a homosexual man who'd found out when he was young that his sexuality made him a potential criminal. I wanted to find out how other homosexual men, some born around the same time as me, some born later, had come to terms with it and dealt with it. So when it was time to talk to people, it was natural I should choose subjects who had experienced the same thing as me – male homosexuality in the United Kingdom when it was illegal, and then after 1967 when it was still legislated against in so many ways.

In Great Britain, female homosexuality has never been against the law. But since 1553 with regard to anal intercourse, and since 1885 with regard to all other forms of sexual activity, male to make sexual activity was a criminal offence until its partial decriminalisation with the *Sexual Offences Act* of 1967. Moreover, increasingly throughout the Fifties, the police had been deliberately entrapping male homosexuals, then prosecuting them. So in the Sixties, the urgent need for a change in the law was a male problem, not a female one. Likewise, the experience of living under the constant threat of arrest and imprisonment simply because of your sexuality.

When I started doing the interviews, my first surprise was the number of well-known people who agreed to participate. My next surprise was just how activist all these people were, so much so it left me feeling that perhaps I'd been rather a lazy gay during these past fifty years. I'd never really suffered from being gay, I'd always been open about my sexuality, and for the most part had thoroughly enjoyed myself. Now, hearing the problems other people had been through, I began to feel a touch guilty at my own charmed life. Should I have done more to help? I'm not sure, because person after person stressed that activism really only requires one thing – that we live openly, gay and uncowed – and that, at least, I'd always done.

Either way, doing the interviews was a huge learning curve for me. And although I found many people who'd suffered severely from the law, I also talked to people who, like myself, had treated the law almost with indifference – we'd avoided the downsides as best we could, tried not to get into trouble, and got on with our lives quite happily. For my part, I think I even quite enjoyed the prejudice, the feeling of being set apart, of being an outsider and not part of the mainstream. And it was because I was in that category that I found it so educational to hear from all those other people.

When I started to talk with the very few lesbians I'd asked to interview, it opened up a new field of interest. I'd love to do another similar project looking, not at the impact of finding yourself a criminal by way of your sexuality, but simply at the impact of homosexuality on your psyche and on your innate personality. But that will have to be another project, another time.

Meanwhile, it's been a super education for me, a real eye-opener. For despite thinking that, as a homosexual, I knew most of it already, I simply didn't. In particular, I enjoyed learning more about trans people. It was an area of homosexuality that I'd never been confronted with and never really understood. The chapter on transitioning is the longest in the book and I found it the most interesting.

The point where I realised perhaps I hadn't spoken to

enough gay women was when I began to edit the interviews about *Section 28*, whereby schools were forbidden to give advice and counselling about homosexuality. As an adult not in the teaching profession, it had little or no impact on me at the time, but while I was editing the interviews I realised that *Section 28* was the first time the law had been used with equal oppression against gay women as gay men. From then on, the fight for equality became their battle too, first with the repeal of *Section 28*, then with the acceptance of gay women and men in the police and military, and lastly with the recognition of gay marriage.

In the end, the overwhelming conclusion I've drawn from all I heard is that it's not so much tolerance that overcomes prejudice but familiarity – letting everyone live their lives the way they want to without feeling the need to interfere – and realising it does no harm to anyone else to let them do so.

ABOUT THE EDITING

As a teenager, I was crazy about jazz. My favourite book was *Hear Me Talkin' To Ya*, a history of jazz edited from hundreds of interviews with famous jazz musicians. I wanted *50 Years Legal* to be done in the same style. But having finished editing the film version of it, which required me to pare away 90 percent of everything that had been said, I found it more difficult than I'd thought to get back into edit mode for a second time. The project languished for a while until my publisher, Mark Neeter, came to the rescue by making an excellent initial cull of the material, nearly 1,000 pages of it. Once that was done, I found myself fired up again and the result is a joint effort.

Thanks, Mark for being such an excellent and patient co-editor.

CHAPTER ONE

Realisations

LEE TRACEY

I was four. I didn't know I was gay of course, it was towards the end of the war and we had this searchlight at the bottom of the street. We used to walk down there, it was only a very small street and first thing in the morning there'd be these soldiers in their underwear. I got a kick out of seeing them like that. I didn't know why.

TOM ROBINSON

I was aware of finding other boys attractive and wanting to be physically close to them long before I had a name for it. I mean it sounds ridiculous but I can actually remember having fantasies age six or seven, that kind of age. I can remember the place I was living at the time and thinking about other boys in that place at that time.

SIMON CALLOW

I knew I was attracted to other boys, or more importantly to men, from a very early age. I knew that I was feeling different things because even at that age kids talk about girls and all the rest of it and I had no interest in that conversation at all. I was very candid about the fact that I found boys attractive and it didn't seem to worry anybody at all. But when you reach a certain age you start wanting to understand yourself and your situation. So I started to read books.

STEPHEN FRY

Books allowed you to believe that you were not the freak that society painted you as. I never imagined I'd be able to have any kind of gay relationship in the way that some of the characters in the books had done. But sometimes there were scenes in a book that would make you go – oh! Like a scene in a Gore Vidal novel that left me kind of flushed and hot.

SIMON CALLOW

I was reading a lot of physiology and so on. I read a famous and probably damaging book called *Homosexuality*, by D. J. West, who was a prison psychiatrist. It was a depressing tale – what it would be like to be gay – for the most part it seemed awful, the depressing nature of gay life.

STEPHEN FRY

It seemed clear that the life one had to look forward to was one of secrecy and silence.

PAUL GAMBACCINI

I didn't even know I was what would now be called gay because there was no frame of reference. But there was a profound sense of aloneness when you realised you were different.

SIMON CALLOW

Life was clearly going to be just utterly depressing, doomed to loneliness and unhappiness; you were going to be ostracised by your fellow human beings and you would get little physical or emotional satisfaction either. It was just disastrous.

ALAIN JUDD

I didn't have any angst about it at all, but I was very lucky in that when I was a boy of 14 I got a job in a record store in the school holidays, and unknown to me all the staff were gay. I was that innocent I didn't know; they were just very nice to me.

DAVID HOCKNEY

The fact it was illegal, you didn't think about that much because you were just having sex with your friends. I knew everybody. I had a good time, actually, when I was young.

MATTHEW PARRIS

My parents listened to Noel Coward and everybody loved Liberace. You could see they were gay and as a boy I found that sort of thing strangely comforting.

ALAIN JUDD

One of the record shop managers had a friend who was also a very distinguished musician and I needed some coaching for my A level composition papers. He was a gay man and we got talking about it and he said, "Well you know, you should never be afraid not to be yourself."

I decided he was probably right so from that moment on I never really thought about it. But then I didn't have to go and work in the local factory.

TOM ROBINSON

When I heard other boys talking about 'homos' at school, it was in such disparaging terms and the worst insult was, "So and so is a homo. Look at him. Look at the way he looks," and so forth.

That's when it dawned on me that those were my feelings too and that I needed to conceal them. It became a very shameful secret. It was the last thing in the world you'd want anyone else to know. And the biggest shame I have is that I joined in pointing the finger at other boys in order to try and draw the heat off me. That's not a good thing to remember.

LORD BROWNE

I was the son of an Auschwitz survivor. All the contexts in which I lived were antithetical to being openly gay. My mother's most important lesson from Auschwitz was never ever entrust anyone with a secret because they will surely let you down.

LEE TRACEY

When I went to secondary modern school there was a boy who used to come and sit next to me and get his dick out and get me to toss him off during maths lessons. Later, when I was 16 I fell in love with this guy at work and I didn't know what to say or how to say it, so I wrote a letter but never posted it. My mother found it in my clothes and that was it.

She blew up one night when I came home from work, called me everything under the sun, took a knife to me and told me to get out the next morning, which I did at 5am.

It was snowing and I took two or three buses to get to where my step-grandmother lived, but I couldn't go and stay with her. I found digs and I lived there, near the guy I was in love with.

TOM ROBINSON

The situation at school of having these secret feelings went into melt down when I fell in love with a boy. I never told him; I would have rather have died than told him or anyone else. But it became a full-blown obsession to the extent of writing his name in note books, surreptitiously trying to take a photo of him out of the classroom window, building up a dossier of all the times I saw him and what he did and what he said, finding when he'd thrown away one of his school books and going to rescue it from the waste paper basket. All this screwed down the lid of the pressure cooker and one day I made a half-hearted attempt to kill myself, because I would rather have died than anyone find out.

LEE TRACEY

I joined the army because there was nothing else to do and I signed up for twelve years because the longer you signed for the more money you got. But after three or four months I couldn't keep the pretence up and I told this other soldier and we slept together. They found me with him in the morning and we were pulled up in front of the camp commander and charged with homosexuality. We were put in separate cells and were both made to run around the parade ground in full pack in pouring rain and freezing cold until you collapsed. Then they'd drag you up and make you run still further. In the end we both got a dishonourable discharge.

TOM ROBINSON

After my suicide attempt, I woke up next morning in the dormitory at school and found out I was still alive. It took two or three seconds to realise I shouldn't have been, then I snapped. I guess I was having a nervous breakdown. It took ten minutes just to get off the bed, get some clothes and go downstairs to breakfast. I was crying uncontrollably and obviously it didn't take long for someone to notice and take me to the headmaster. He said "What's the trouble?" and it all came pouring out.

That afternoon I was taken to a mental hospital in Cambridge and they medicalised the situation. The thing about homosexuality as it was presented to me was – it was a sin, it was a crime, and it was a disease, and in this instance they took the disease option. I was made to put on my pyjamas and get into bed. They took my temperature and they filled me full of drugs – a kind of chemical cosh. Then the white coated psychiatrists came round and showed me ink-block tests and asked me loads of damn fool questions about what I felt – really stupid sophistry.

They said, "So what makes you think you're a homosexual?"

"The fact I'm in love with this other boy," I told them.

They asked, "Yes, but have you actually had sex with him?"

"Of course I bloody haven't," I told them, "I haven't had sex with anybody."

So they said, "Well in that case you're not a homosexual. You see, a homosexual is somebody who actually has sex with somebody of the same gender. So in fact you aren't a homosexual."

What help is that to a desperate, lonely, teenager at the end of his tether in a hospital ward being filled with drugs, just aching to get out of the hospital and kill himself properly?

LEE TRACEY

I went to Leeds but I couldn't get any work, couldn't find anybody, and had no money, so I ended up trying to take my own life, cutting my wrists. I was found by a police car about half-past-four in the morning, practically frozen to death on the side of a road. Later, they took me to an infirmary where I was sectioned and eventually they put me in a padded room. They brought a trolley with drinks on it and asked what drinks I like? They gave me whisky and this guy, this nurse, put a tape recorder next to the bed and injected me and the injection worked against the whisky and made me sick and vomit while the tape recorder is playing, telling me what a filthy creature I am and how disgusting my life is.

This was going on and on for three days and three nights — no food, no water, nothing but this whisky and the injection until I banged on the door and screamed that I was cured, that I was straight.

They got me out, cleaned me up and to cut a long story short I went home with a police woman and went to bed with her, the very first time I'd been in bed with a woman. I ended up living with her, even marrying her, and we had a baby. Then everything went wrong again. I couldn't keep up the pretence.

TOM ROBINSON

After I'd been in the psychiatric wing of the hospital in Cambridge for some weeks my authoritarian dad came and visited me. He said briskly, "Don't worry, we'll soon get you out of here and back to your A Levels."

I said, "Dad, when I get out of here I'm going to do the job properly – kill myself for good."

And this stern father just crumpled in front of my eyes. I'd never seen anything like it. He started crying and this white stuff came out of his tear ducts because he hadn't used them in so long, and he just crumpled onto the bed and sobbed, "I don't want to lose you."

It was the first time I'd realised this patriarch actually loved me and cared about me.

LEE TRACEY

I had to leave my wife. I'd met a guy. I'd been out shopping or something; I'd gone into a toilet and a guy there had picked me up. It was just masturbation, but I was running a newsagent's shop at the time and later, after this incident, by some quirk of fate he came in when I was behind the counter and recognised me.

He tried to blackmail me and I gave him money until it got out of hand. I thought if I didn't pay the money he'd not only tell my wife but the police and everybody else, and I couldn't face it. So I packed a case, wrote a note, and left my wife and child and went to Brighton. Then later to Newquay.

TOM ROBINSON

The beginning of the light at the end of the tunnel came at the start of the following year when my headmaster got me an interview at Finchden Manor, a therapeutic community for disturbed adolescents in Kent, and arranged for my dad to take me down there. I didn't know what I was going into, nor did he.

We had a four-hour drive and rolled up in this courtyard at an Elizabethan manor house with the kind of windows that had been broken and mended, then broken and mended, again and again. There was a row of unkempt hairy faces at the windows staring at us as we pulled up in the courtyard and I was shown into an oak panel study where there was a 73-year-old man with a stoop and dirty plastic-rimmed glasses and an old sports jacket. He came up to me and took my hand in both of his and held it for longer than felt comfortable. He peered over the top of his glasses at me and said, "Hello! You're very lonely aren't you." And I knew I'd come home.

This was the place I'd known I ought to be. This was someone who cut through all the ink-block tests and drugs and psychiatric bullshit and went straight to the heart of the matter – that I was a completely isolated individual living in a word of total fantasy, separated from my real self.

I knew this was somebody who understood where I was hurting and knew how to make the hurting stop.

LEE TRACEY

In Newquay there was an RAF camp just outside the town. I met a guy there and we had a secret affair. He was in the RAF but he got killed in a car crash about a year later. So I left again. I didn't know where I was going, I just left. I even had a dog there and left my dog and I would never leave a dog. I'm a dog lover, but I did; I was so beside myself. My friend who got killed was the only person in Newquay who knew I was gay.

I ended up walking in the pouring rain with a carrier bag all the way to Plymouth, where I found some digs and eventually got a job in a hotel as a breakfast and veg chef. I'd never cooked breakfast or veg in my life but I stayed there until it just got too much. Then I ended up in London, and there I found somebody.

SIMON CALLOW

I was quite a late starter because I could never find anybody to have sex with because I didn't go to a public school. I was at a grammar school and I couldn't see any gay people there at all as far as I knew. I sort of flirted with a young woman and I really just didn't want to do it, it didn't appeal to me at all. To be gay was clearly going to be utterly depressing – doomed to loneliness and unhappiness, and you were going to be ostracized by your fellow human beings. I felt very strongly there was nothing I could do about it – it looked as though celibacy was the only option.

TOM ROBINSON

It was at Finchden Manor, in a closed community of fifty young men, that I first slept with somebody of the same sex – well, that I first slept with anybody for that matter. It was something people kind of knew about but nobody cared one way or the other. Interesting that twenty or thirty percent of the boys were absolutely heterosexual and were not remotely interested in the kind of attraction that happens in prisons or other places where men are confined together. If you made a pass at them they'd just laugh, "Don't be so silly, I don't fancy you, go away," with no up-tightness about it.

Then there were the ones who went, "Oh no! Backs against the walls, chaps."

They were the ones who would sooner or later hop into bed and experiment with someone during the course of their stay there, then move on. Kind of like public school, I'm guessing.

STEPHEN FRY

I was at public school. All gay things interested me when I was a teenager but obviously, because it was forbidden and it was a secret thing, I knew if anybody found out I would be in terrible trouble. I imagined I'd grow up living a life like some of the political scandals I read about, like Oscar Wilde. That I'd have to escape Britain and live in Capri or North Africa or whatever.

LORD PADDICK

When I was born, homosexuality was illegal in the UK and when on the rare occasion discussions about homosexuality came up at home my parents made very clear what their views were and it was very hostile.

LEE TRACEY

I can't say I was glad to have been born when I was – it was a miserable existence for gay people then. Maybe not for everybody, but I didn't know anybody, so for me it was. And what they did to me in hospital in Leeds ruined my life because I got married and had a daughter, and I not only ruined my own life but ruined my daughter's life too. So I loathe what they did to me, and what they did to other people too – thousands of other people, not just gay people but ordinary people with a mental problem – they gave them electric shock treatment. I saw these people walking around the wards looking like zombies, and I *mean* zombies. That was a terrible, terrible thing.

MARC ALMOND

Homosexuality was made legal when I was ten years of age. I didn't actually realise what homosexuality was, but whether it was illegal or legal or whatever it was, when I was at school I knew I had strong attachments to boys, maybe what we would call unhealthy attachments, obsessive attachments, so I knew that there was something kind of different about me. But like you did at that time, you kind of invented girlfriends and believed you had these girlfriends. You were in this kind of denial, and invented this kind of protection around you.

SIR DEREK JACOBI

I spent three years at the Birmingham repertory company. I hadn't been to drama school so that was my training ground and I was also finding my way sexually. There was one leading lady in the company whom I literally had to throw out of the flat one night because she chased me around the room screaming she would turn me on or whatever. But there was never a great problem for me, I had accepted it from that start. I knew that's how I was born.

MARK WARDEL

I was brought up in New Brighton in the North of England, a seaside place by Liverpool. You know you're different even from an early age. You don't really know what it is but you have this kind of feeling of difference and a bit of displacement. Then gradually, as you get to 13 or 14, you start to realize you're not interested in girls, you're kind of interested in guys.

At that time, in the early Seventies, there were no gay role models and everyone was having to live this lie and pretend that they weren't gay. As far as I knew I was the only gay person in the entire place. It was something I had to keep to myself.

LEE TRACEY

In London I started doing something I really enjoyed – entertaining as a stand-up comedian. An agent said to me, "You know, you ought to do drag."

In those days we weren't called drag acts we were called female impersonators. I have some pictures of when I was first in drag, I looked like hell. I'm leaning against the doorpost of a place where I used to live in Teddington and I'm wearing this long purple frock. I look like Languid Lil from Stamford Hill.

JULIAN CLARY

My sister was a glamour dancer so I used to go and sit in her dressing room at a formative age and watch her put on all this makeup.

LORD CASHMAN

I knew I was gay from an early age. I knew that girls were my friends, and boys were the common enemy to be loved and admired, but from afar. Sadly, as a working-class boy I picked up my stories through the salacious Sunday papers, vicars and others who were seen to 'prey' on young boys. I used to think – if only they would prey upon me

LORD BROWNE

I decided, very simply, that I would create two lives – a public life people saw, and a private life that would be in so far as was possible in the shadowy world of gay life. And I would participate carefully.

STEVE BLAME

I came from a small village and I used to look up at the stars and really wish I could leave this planet and go to another.

CHAPTER TWO

Decriminalisation

STEPHEN FRY

While I was at school there was a famous case involving Lord Montagu of Beaulieu and a man who became something of a hero of mine called Peter Wildeblood. He and Lord Montagu were arrested with others supposedly for having various sexual relations on a beach in Sussex. They all pleaded not guilty except Peter Wildeblood, who pleaded guilty and went to prison. He was probably one of the first people to come out as gay.

SIR DEREK JACOBI

I was fascinated when I read about Peter Wildeblood, I was also frightened, and outraged too. These people were demonstrating what I was and they were being persecuted and hounded for it. And sent to prison.

LORD CASHMAN

For me, one of the pivotal moments was the Peter Wildeblood/Lord Montagu case. Here was a combustible mix of a peer of the realm, a television executive, and some men from the RAF, which exploded, not only as you would expect in the *News of the World*, but around Whitehall. And this directly, or maybe indirectly, lead into the *Wolfenden Report*, which Churchill commissioned to look into homosexuality and prostitution.

STEPHEN FRY

One of the problems with the *Wolfenden Report* was that it was being conducted by rather well-meaning bureaucrats and civil servants who could find no one to come forward and describe their experiences. But then Peter Wildeblood agreed, and he spoke very emotionally and powerfully about the experiences of being a gay man.

PETER TATCHELL

The *Wolfenden Report* was a real breakthrough in that

it recommended at least a partial decriminalisation of homosexuality. But John Wolfenden is not the saint that he is often portrayed as. He was in fact the main obstacle to a much more progressive report. Many other members of his committee wanted more liberal recommendations, including an equalisation of the age of consent. But Wolfenden blocked that. He said if you insist on this I will resign and the committee will fold, so he basically blackmailed other committee members to agree to his more hardline recommendations.

Even so, when the government appointed John Wolfenden they saw him as a safe pair of hands. Their expectation had been that he would recommend new measures to control and constrain gay and bisexual men; they were not expecting him to recommend even the limited partial decriminalisation that he ultimately proposed.

LORD CASHMAN

Churchill commissioned the *Wolfenden Report* but didn't act on its recommendations because there was no agreement from his home secretary. Churchill left office within a couple of years, but that kind of social reform needed a Labour government to bring it forward, and it needed a free vote in the House. The fact that it started life as a private member's bill suited everyone. But I think Harold Wilson quite rightly saw that it was of its time, and so did Roy Jenkins. I give Wilson a lot of credit because he had to steer the cabinet. I don't dress up any political party as being more progressive than the other; each political party had progressives and conservatives. But Wilson took them on and said, "This is absolutely the right thing to do."

STEPHEN FRY

Yes, there were political figures who fought for what they

believed in, but always you know it's artists and people in popular culture who make the most difference. In 1961 there was a British film called *Victim* with Dirk Bogarde – and my goodness the courage of Bogarde who was a huge star for the Rank Organisation at the time and was adored by women like my mother because he played Dr. Simon Sparrow in *Doctor in the House* and was a handsome devil.

In *Victim* he was playing a barrister who was clearly gay, and indeed 'queer' was the word that was scrawled up on his garage door in the movie. And when his wife finds out about him he has this wonderful speech, "I wanted him. I wanted him. Alright?"

You can laugh at it because it's such a very English film, but gosh does it still pack a punch! The law was a charter for blackmailers and in the film you saw two creepy blackmailers who because of it were able to threaten to destroy careers of people and suck them dry of money, with resulting suicides.

Bogarde is greatly to be thanked for doing it because what was so important about the film was that it wasn't just a sympathetic portrait of a gay person, it highlighted the wickedness of the law.

ANGELA EAGLE

Simply because the law made it illegal, gay men were in a particularly difficult situation. There was a lot of deliberate blackmail taking place. It made people's lives very haunted.

SIMON CALLOW

There were endless political scandals going on in the early Sixties and one of them concerned a rather insignificant naval attaché who worked for the Navy in Moscow called William Vassall. I couldn't read enough about William Vassall because he was a gay man, and I wanted to know more about the lives of gay men. They'd caught him passing secrets to the Russians by sending a rather pretty Russian policeman to seduce him. What I was mainly shocked about was that the newspapers were eager to supply all the detail about the sexual examination of William Vassall. They made it so distasteful, but I was absolutely fascinated. How they had done rectal probes and things like that, and how his very name seemed so like Vaseline, some kind of terrible gay parody.

LORD CASHMAN

In the end the change in the law came about, I believe, not only because of the *Wolfenden Report* and the Wildeblood/Montagu case, but from all those women and men who went to prison, or who lost their life or their liberty, because they wouldn't conform.

STEPHEN K. AMOS

I think we all have to remember the people who've gone on before us where it was very much a political statement where it was about people's lives that mattered. Those people didn't have a chance to blow a whistle or have rainbow flags or wear next to nothing marching up and down the street – they were abused and spat at. Those people put their lives on the line to make it possible.

PETER TATCHELL

One of the first positive outcomes from the *Wolfenden Report* was the formation in the following year, 1958, of the Homosexual Law Reform Society. This was the first campaign group to work for law reform to get the Wolfenden report implemented. It was very London focused but all the gay members were closeted. It primarily sought to get the great and the good on side, so bishops and other public figures were very much part of its campaign agenda. But most of the MPs and Lords who backed law reform in 1967 did so begrudgingly. The underlying tone to their support was that these gay people were poor pitiable creatures and we mustn't persecute them, they suffer this terrible affliction. That was the kind of mentality that drove a lot of the support in parliament for law reform. It wasn't acceptance or understanding. It wasn't true support.

MATTHEW PARRIS

Before 1967, male homosexuality had been completely illegal in Britain and people regularly went to prison for it. The decriminalisation, while admittedly not covering everybody, at least covered consenting adults over 21. It was a terrific thing.

PETER TATCHELL

In fact, it wasn't a true decriminalisation, it only meant that same sex activity between men was not prosecuted providing both men were aged 21 or over, which was five years higher than the heterosexual age of consent, and only providing the sexual acts took place in the privacy of their own homes with doors and windows locked, the curtains drawn and no other person present in any other part of the house.

If I invited friends of mine down to London from Manchester to stay in my flat in my spare room knowing that they were gay and likely to have sex, I was committing the criminal offence of aiding and abetting. And they were committing the criminal offence of having sex in premises where more than two people were present.

LORD CASHMAN

It was only decriminalised in 'private' circumstances. And the definition of 'private' meant in your own home. It couldn't be at a friend's house because anyone could come in at any time.

If you went out into public cruising areas, that was an offence under the *Sexual Offences Act*. And that continued right through to the Nineties and was only finally repealed in 2003. The message to the gay and bisexual community was clear, "You can do it, but you do it in private, and you don't talk about it."

TOM ROBINSON

There was an offence called 'gross indecency' which only applied to men and it covered a whole range of conduct from a male on male kiss in a public place through to, obviously, cottaging or what have you, but it didn't apply to women, and it didn't apply to men and women together. Convictions for gross indecency actually rose by two hundred percent after 1967. The police were using it as *carte blanche* to get easy arrests and build up their careers.

PAUL GAMBACCINI

In the Seventies the police were still arresting gay people, often for almost no reason. For instance, using the 'pretty police'.

In London, the youngest best-looking police were tarted up and sent into public parks and public lavatories to entice gay men into making propositions, at which point they would be arrested. Thousands of people were arrested in this way and every morning the police would bring them to the magistrates' court, boasting of having done a good night's work. They were just harvesting gay people.

PETER TATCHELL

In the early Seventies there were certain pubs and restaurants that would refuse to serve gay people. So, modeled on the tactics of the black civil rights movement in the United States, the Gay Liberation Front organised sit-ins in these venues. One particularly famous one was at the Chepstow Pub in West London. About 50 of us went there one night to demand to be served and when the landlord refused we sat down and occupied the pub. Within 20 minutes the police arrived, not one or two policemen but several police van loads and we were violently ejected. Some of us were put in the alleyway where we were strip searched. I can remember a burly sergeant putting his hands in my underpants and squeezing my testicles until I screamed. That was the kind of sadism that was common in the police. But we did win the battle. Eventually the Chepstow realised we would never go away and after about four weeks it allowed us to enter and we were served.

LEE TRACEY

I had a gig doing a drag act in a pub in the West End, then another at another pub. In those days you could park in the West End so I drove to the second gig still in drag, parked my car and walked across the pavement to the front door of the pub. But before I could pass through it I was arrested.

"Offending public morals", that was the charge they quoted me, just for walking across the pavement in drag. And I was thrown into a police cell for the night.

The next morning I had to appear in Bow Street magistrates' court where I was fined five guineas – as much as I earned a night in those days – just for walking across the pavement in drag. And it wasn't a pleasant feeling standing there in the dock with my overnight beard coming through the makeup and the magistrate looked at me with, you know, disdain.

ALAIN JUDD

The police used to hide in the cubicles at public conveniences. If a man went in for a pee and smiled or spoke to the person next to them, the policeman would jump out of the cubicle and say he was under arrest. He'd be held until the next morning, then appear in the magistrates' court.

PETER TATCHELL

In the years after the 1967 act the number of convictions of gay and bisexual men increased by nearly 400 percent compared to the prosecution level in 1965 or 1966. It was as if the state was giving us some concessions while saying you're not getting an inch more. The remaining laws were enforced with an even greater ferocity.

SIR DEREK JACOBI

That frightened me, and it didn't make me want to go out there and wave a fist, I was too timid. It upset me deeply but I still didn't want to face head on that it was part of me, that it was mine. Why go out there and share it and say accept me? No, I had accepted myself and that was enough for me.

MATTHEW PARRIS

I never got any pleasure from the secret knowledge I was different from the straight people who were around me. I never got any pleasure from the idea that I was part of a secret club. I just hated the dishonesty. And mostly, the practical problems of being gay just irritated me. Although I knew I was gay, I really didn't notice the 1967 act at the time.

TOM ROBINSON

For many gay men the 1967 act was a huge step forward, for others it hardly made any difference. For some people, though, it seemed to make matters worse. The police became worryingly out of order. For instance, men could be arrested for a male on male kiss. It meant at least a fine if not a small prison sentence. Although legalisation had technically happened there were so many men going to prison for consensual sex, it was a nightmare.

PETER TATCHELL

You had the absurd situation where two gay men who booked into a hotel and had sex together overnight were committing a criminal act because the hotel was deemed not to be a private place and the hotel could be prosecuted for aiding and abetting a homosexual act. Likewise, if two men queuing at a supermarket checkout fancied each other, started chatting, and exchanged names and phone numbers, that was deemed to be importuning for a homosexual act which was illegal and punishable by up to two years imprisonment.

All these laws, including the law that sent Oscar Wilde to prison in 1895, remained on the statute books under the heading 'unnatural offences'. It's only very recently that criminalisation of homosexuality has truly been ended, with the *Sexual Offences Act of 2003*.

CHAPTER THREE

Testing the waters

JON SAVAGE

There was a generational divide between post-war people, who didn't care about the law, and those who came earlier. Somebody who I would call a Thirties person, who was born up to 1939-40, would be very different from someone born during the war or after 1945. The later generation didn't give a fuck that homosexuality was illegal. It was to do with the culture, to do with changing attitudes, to do with the end of the Victorians.

I always think the end of Victorianism was Winston Churchill's funeral in early 1965. That was the end of it. And that was when the Sixties kicked in, with the Beatles and everything.

SIR DEREK JACOBI

Yeah, the Beatles and everything. I suppose I was typical of my age and my time. I did the gay clubs.

ALAIN JUDD

There was one club on the Kings Road – the Gigolo. It was dark and you went downstairs where there was a little person behind a hole in the wall and they stamped your hand when you paid. I've forgotten how much it was, almost nothing in those days, and there was Coca Cola or coffee, certainly no booze.

SIR DEREK JACOBI

At the Gigolo, you went downstairs and it was always very crowded. I think the way to describe my personality is 'timid'. So when I went to these clubs I was usually a waiting violet, watching everybody else get off but rarely did I venture. I did occasionally, but I didn't meet the love of my life in those places. They were fun, but there was also the feeling they were dangerous, which frightened me and yet attracted me.

ALAIN JUDD

Gay clubs were great social levellers. Like being a glamorous girl, being gay sometimes gave you entry into a society to which you were not born. Lords and lorry drivers could cavort together, which in straight society they generally didn't.

MATTHEW PARRIS

There were certain designated gay pubs and everybody knew which ones they were and for a while I got into the gay sub culture that existed. It was for me very liberating because that was the only time I could be with people where I could speak freely, but It was also quite limiting because you found yourself just standing around in a pub talking with a few people whom you didn't really know very well.

ALAIN JUDD

There were other gay places too, like the Turkish baths. The Royal Opera House crowd always enjoyed the Savoy Baths in Jermyn Street. If you had a show in the evening and had done rehearsal in the morning, in the afternoon you'd have free time on your hands. So a whole band of us, a whole cohort, would go off to the steam baths and have a great giggle. The dancers were particularly keen on them because not only could they ease their aching muscles, but if they were lucky there might be a bit of slap and tickle to be had. We nicknamed that place the 'Wheel of Fortune'.

MATTHEW PARRIS

Looking back on those years I think it's possible to exaggerate what fun the gay social scene was at least for most people. There may have been some people who went to marvellous parties and knew lots of other exotically gay people and had a jolly good time, but for most of us it was all a bit furtive, a bit limiting.

ALAIN JUDD

In the green belts around London were the cruising places like Tooting Beck Common, Clapham Common, and Chelsea Graveyard, where you could go and flip between bodies, and Hampstead Heath. The attraction was the danger, I think. It was exciting.

If you went into a public loo you'd get to see witty pictures and words written on the cubicle doors. Sometimes you could laugh yourself silly. Once I saw a Christian cross on the door and written below it was, "Lord forgive them for they know not what they do."

Underneath, someone had written, "Yes, we fucking well do."

During the weekend there was The Vauxhall Tavern, in Vauxhall, and the East End pub in docklands owned by a famous broadcaster, Dan Farson. It was very seedy, but there were lots of famous people. We met Noel Coward there, for instance. It was run by a fearful old queen who really had the power. We called her Stella Minge, and Stella looked after all the sailors and took care of any trouble, because, if you got a bunch of bananas from him you wouldn't get up. He was always in mild drag, not proper drag but trousers that were a little bit too flared for a man in those days.

LORD CASHMAN

If you were lucky enough to live somewhere like Manchester or London, where you could get into the anonymous middle of the city, you could go to gay bars. But if you were a teacher living in Trafford, or a young brickie who lived in East Ham, it was completely different, because you had to live and operate in the world of your mates and your family. That was the destructive element of the criminalisation – the stigmatisation and persecution of gay men and bisexuals. If you stepped outside of the box that you were born into and supposed to grow within... If you dared to step outside of that box, then the full weight of the law would be brought upon you.

Equally, people who frequented gay pubs in the city centre were terrified that someone would walk in who knew them. They didn't make the connection that, if they were in the bar as well, they might also be gay. People lived with a certain amount of fear. Even though I was a young actor, I didn't know anyone who was successful who was gay. I knew people who were in the closet – in fact they weren't in the closet, they were in nuclear bunkers – terrified of how it might affect their career, especially if they were the handsome young leading man. Though if they were the camp comic, nobody seemed to give a damn.

SIMON CALLOW

Around that time I went to see a woman who was supposed to dispel various ailments and told her I had a problem with hay fever. She asked, "Are you a homosexual?"

I told her, "Yes, I am a homosexual."

She said, "Why are so many homosexuals so unhappy?"

I answered, "Do you think it might have something to do with the way other people treat them in society?'"

'No,' she insisted, "You've got to block it. Now sit down."

She did cure my hay fever, but she didn't cure my homosexuality.

LEE TRACEY

In London we used to go to a tea wagon on The Embankment. All the queens went there, and all the female impersonators. It was next to a public toilet and we'd stand there till three o'clock in the morning, pissed out of our brains drinking a flask of gin or whatever. We called it the Starlight Roofs. In those days you got picked up at those places.

ALAIN JUDD

I already had a boyfriend while I was still at school in the Sixties – Barrie. And we used to go to the gay pubs together in Earls Court.

At school we had a master, the assistant director of music, who was a distinguished musician and the conductor of a big London choir. One night at a gay pub called The Boltons I went to the loo. When I came back, there was our assistant director of music standing at the bar, almost next to my friend. He said, "Oh, hello. What are you doing here then?" Very Welsh.

I said, "I could ask you the same thing, couldn't I, sir?"

Of course, when I saw him the next day at school nothing was said. It was all very under wraps, you know.

LEE TRACEY

Well, a friend of mine, Ronnie Ellis, got picked up by two Irish guys and they murdered him. They took him back to his place in West Ham, cut off his private parts off and shoved them in his mouth, then murdered him. He was found by the milkman who saw them getting out the window because he'd locked the door from the inside. They had all his stuff piled up. They were going to nick it but they couldn't take it out because he'd put the door on the lock. They did catch them though.

ALAIN JUDD

We were once in The Cricketers, a gay pub in Battersea Park Road, when Rudolf Nureyev swanned in, all in leather including a big leather cap and flowing hair. He went to the bar, pulled off his cap, and shook out his hair like a mane. Then posed.

It was like bees to a honey pot but he pretended he didn't like it. It was all just for show.

SIMON CALLOW

I still didn't quite see how I fitted in. It's a curious thing, it's to do with self-image and all of that. There were stereotypes of gay people that you could see all around, full-out drag queens, or people like Larry Grayson on the television, but it didn't do anything for me at all. I was still worried that life would be rather terrible, and when I went to work in the box-office of the Old Vic Theatre in 1967 the box-office manager had in his safe a copy of *Last Exit to Brooklyn*, the shock book of the day, about drag queens. He said, "You'd better read this book. It's all about queers and the way they pick up jolly bags in the park and suck them." It was just so disgusting and terrible.

But then I went to drama school and started meeting people who were just normally gay. Miraculously and extraordinarily I suddenly found I was having sex, and it was just wonderfully exciting.

SIR DEREK JACOBI

What drama school showed me was that there were lots of others like me, and I felt safe. I felt secure because of the tolerance you found. In the world of the arts, the tolerance is amazing, and even before there was any legislation, even before you'd confessed to yourself you weren't like other people, long before all of that, it was taken for granted that they knew. It was what you did, who you were, how you treated other people. That was what was important, not your sexuality.

SIMON CALLOW

I was now discovering how to act. At first it wasn't clear I could act at all. It seemed I had no instincts for it. I was too rigid. But once I'd discovered sex I became a different person completely. My whole centre shifted and I was able to give in to the impulses of an act, or a character, and to reveal myself in all kinds of ways. I could show anger, I could show lust, I could show cruelty, I could show affection – all of these things without inhibition.

TOM ROBINSON

It was around then that I arrived in London. There was something called Gay Switchboard, which for me was a lifeline. They told me about an upcoming gay ball organised by the Gay Liberation Front at the Surrey Halls in Stockwell, not far from where I was living.

When the day came I put on my glad rags and went there, but outside was a gang of youths loitering by the door and I thought – oh Christ, now I'm in for trouble.

As I got closer I saw they were all wearing GLF badges. They were the welcoming committee of the Gay Liberation Front, and inside there was a stall with loads more badges and leaflets and stuff. Then we went upstairs and it was like all the school discos I'd ever known where someone would borrow a couple of turntables and get a home-made amplifier and people would bring their own records, and everyone would sit around the outside of the dance floor, all looking at each other, the boys too shy to ask the girls to dance, the girls too shy to catch a boy's eye. Except here, no one seemed shy at all. And the boys were dancing with the boys and the girls were dancing with the girls.

I suddenly had this huge, amazing, life-changing, realisation that you could see somebody you fancy and go up to them and say, "Do you want to dance?" And it suddenly dawned on me, that's what dancing was about.

Up to that point I'd thought it was like football, one of those inexplicable things that straight people did – you got up on the dance floor, you danced, you sat down again – but why would you want do that?

Well of course – because you fancy the other person!

For that startling revelation I felt indebted to the Gay Liberation Front. And from thereon I was a firm believer in its principal and most essential message Come out.

SIMON CALLOW

At drama school, partly because of sex and partly because of acting, I became as it were, myself. I realised the absolutely most important thing any gay person can do is to come out. It's the starting point, the absolute base for everything. From that point and beyond you can do all sorts of necessary and useful things, even politically.

PETER TATCHELL

The partial decriminalisation of male homosexuality had opened the space where people felt less afraid of coming out because unless they got caught in the obscure minutiae of the ongoing illegality they were free to be gay. Shortly after I arrived in London in 1971, I joined the Gay Liberation Front, which had not long been formed. The distinctive thing about it was that it was not defensive or apologetic. It was defiant. We were not victims. We were going to fight for our rights and people would have to accept us on our terms.

TOM ROBINSON

There was plenty to fight for. The metropolitan police were behaving completely out of order. They'd go to Earls Court where there was a popular gay pub called The Coleherne. At closing time when people came out onto the street, the police would arrest them for obstructing the highway or on suspicion of committing a crime. They beat people up and bundled them into the backs of vans and things.

PETER TATCHELL

The Gay Liberation Front was really unique. We had an agenda that went way beyond equality and law reform. For us homosexuality wasn't the problem, it was society that was the problem. We wanted to change society and change the culture. We wanted to get rid of homophobia and make life better for all LGBT people.

TOM ROBINSON

It went beyond just LGBT people. The GLF manifesto was saying gay liberation is everybody's liberation. You either live in a free and fair and equal society or you don't.

PETER TATCHELL

The first *Gay Pride* march was in 1972. I helped organise and publicise it. Less than one thousand people turned out and we were flanked virtually by a police officer for every single marcher. They hemmed us in and some of the officers openly shouted homophobic abuse. In those days there was nothing we could do. You know we felt like we were being treated like criminals, which in the eyes of the law we often still were. But for the first time, hundreds of LGBT people came out and marched and protested. We were demanding nothing less than our full emancipation.

ANGELA EAGLE

Totally by accident, when I was about 17, I was in London. I was a chess player and I was down playing chess. I'd gone out to have a bit of a run between rounds of a vicious competition and I came across a very early version of the *Pride* march. It was quite small, and full of the angst of cowling police officers in full uniform. Just a few people, you know, trying to have fun. But absolutely nobody dressing up.

I saw it go past, and when you think about that, and then

you think about the carnival that is *Pride* now, it sums up the changes we've seen since the Seventies, and who wouldn't want to celebrate that?

SIMON CALLOW

I wasn't on the first of the gay marches but I was on several subsequent ones and at first we were all very anxious, everybody was very anxious, the police were anxious, and they were out in force because they didn't know what would happen. At first people looked at us kind of curiously – at what homosexuals looked like *en masse*. Then they said, "Oh they seem to be having fun," and bit-by-bit they started joining in.

PETER TATCHELL

After that first *Gay Pride* march we went for a picnic in Hyde Park and played gay versions of children games like oranges and lemons and spin the bottle, and there was kissing and you could see the lines of police that ringed around us standing there grim faced with arms folded. But there were so many of us they couldn't do anything and that was incredible.

LORD CASHMAN

On the first *Gay Pride* march we had two different chants. As we walked along Oxford Street we shouted, "We're here, we're queer and we're not going shopping," though sadly a few people did in fact peel off and go to the shops.

The other chant was aimed at the police, who were in a really bad mood because they had to march alongside us. The call was, "Two, four, six, eight – is that copper really straight?"

And we never got an answer.

PAUL GAMBACCINI

I went on one of the early *Gay Pride* marches and felt a little nervous what the public reaction would be. Ian McKellen said to me, "OK, we're going to march through central London, don't worry, wave. Because if you wave at everybody they'll instinctively wave back. And they can't curse you if they're waving at you."

He was right. We marched down Piccadilly and through the centre of London and we were all waving as if we were returning astronauts and people leaned out their windows and waved back. So ingenious.

PETER TATCHELL

Famously the police started putting flowers in their helmets and all the rest of it and suddenly I concluded then, which I maintain and have always maintained, that despite occasional nasty setbacks, essentially British people rather like their gays. They like us and find us entertaining and colourful, and sort of talented and different and unusual. But of course, there are always pockets of resistance and hatred, but that's true of anybody. It's true of Jews or the disabled or wherever there's a kind of fear or dread. The Gay Liberation Front adopted the word gay as a short, simple, non-medical, non-sexual term, and for us it embraced everyone – lesbian, gay, bisexual, transgender, intersects, the whole lot. It was only later that 'gay' came to be more commonly associated with gay men, but in the days of the Gay Liberation Front that wasn't the case.

TOM ROBINSON

Back then, 'gay' meant L-G-B-T-Q all the way down the alphabet. It was *everybody*. It was an inclusive term that meant men, women, the undecided, the indeterminate – people of every conceivable gender. It was everything that wasn't straight, heterosexual or normative kind of behaviour, and that was really liberating. Just three letters said it all, 'G. A. Y.'

CHAPTER FOUR

Bowie shows the way

JON SAVAGE

It's important to realise that in the Sixties a lot of British show-business and in particular the music industry was run by old queens, or even middle-aged queens. The head of EMI, Sir Joseph Lockwood, was gay; the head of Decca, Edward Lewis, was gay; and a lot of managers and agents were too. the Beatles were managed by a gay man, Brian Epstein, and it's strange to look back and think that the biggest phenomenon in the world at the time was managed by a gay man. It's inevitable that some of his gay consciousness must have seeped into the way the Beatles presented themselves and maybe even the songs they wrote.

By the time the Seventies arrived you had Rod Stewart, Elton John, Marc Bolan and David Bowie, all of whom had been scuffling around since the mid-Sixties in a music industry saturated with gay people. And Dusty Springfield, who in 1970 was the first major pop star to come out as gay.

STEPHEN FRY

The year 1972 was incredibly important to me. I was 15 and there were these political things going on, but also it was when we started to get the explosion of glam rock and what was variously called gender bending, with characters like Bowie, Elton John and Marc Bolan. There were so many of these glittery and sexually ambiguous figures who began to point down the *Top of the Pops* camera and beckon with their finger. Kids like me were going, "Oh my gosh."

We could smell the danger, the sexuality, the sensuality, the real excitement of it.

JON SAVAGE

Bowie was absolutely central to the whole story. His interview with *Melody Maker* in January 1972 was the key moment. It was five years after homosexuality had been partially decriminalised and he said, "I'm gay, hello."

A door opens, and nobody is ever going to close it.

TRIS PENNA

I've still got that copy of *Melody Maker*. It was very important for me. Before the internet, culture was where all our messages came from.

LORD CASHMAN

Music and popular culture drove the political agenda.

STEPHEN FRY

I was astonished by this idea that someone could say to a journalist that they were homosexual. I couldn't imagine having the courage to come out.

All these very straight fans of Bowie, who had gone into school colouring their hair and cutting it like *Aladdin Sane*, were none-the-less absolutely shocked at the idea he might actually be gay. As Bowie fans they worried that people might perceive them too to be gay. So they said, "No, he's bisexual."

Other people said, "No, it's a marketing ploy."

JON SAVAGE

Then he did the famous *Top of the Pops* appearance with 'Starman' and 'John, I'm Only Dancing'. And then everybody was away, really.

The thing about Bowie is that he came out as gay. Whether or not he was gay, whether or not he was bisexual, doesn't matter because it's pop music, and it's an area of play and experimentation and fantasy. After Bowie came out as gay he had hits, so it didn't kill off his career, and what Bowie did was he unleashed glam rock, which of course in retrospect was fast, furious, terrific, and fun.

MARC ALMOND

Firstly, there was glam rock. You could hide behind glam rock. You could wear makeup for the first time, you could express yourself with coloured hair or clothes that you wore, and nobody thought necessarily you could be gay, you could just be into glam rock. Then you had punk, and post-punk, and new romantics, and disco, and all these kinds of things. The Seventies really enabled you to have disguises.

WILL YOUNG

What's so great about being a gay artist is you know you can be really subversive and you can have different layers that can be spotted by different people.

MARK WARDEL

When David Bowie came out and said, "I'm gay," the normal trajectory for a pop star was straight, bisexual, then gay, but he did it the wrong way around. He was gay, then bisexual, then straight. But when he came out and said he was gay, he was the coolest person you'd ever seen. It really made a difference to me and a lot of people from my generation.

STEVE BLAME

I was 13 when Bowie announced he was gay. For me this was obviously very impactful because I was a teenager and had also started to have feelings for the same sex. Going to a Bowie concert was the first time in my life that I'd seen all these wonderful people that I wanted to be a part of – wonderfully flamboyant people, women with women, men with men. Suddenly I thought – wow, there's a world out there for me and it isn't this fucking horrible little village where I'm growing up. It was a very important moment in my life.

TRIS PENNA

Because I was late in applying to college I couldn't go to halls of residence so I had to live in a room on a council estate run by a woman who was an Irish Catholic. I was there for one term and when I came back, because I had a David Bowie poster on my wall I was immediately asked to leave, they didn't want gay people living there. Just because I had a David Bowie poster on my wall.

MARK WARDEL

My friends Derick and Simon were barmen at Legends nightclub. One night I was at my flat and got a phone call from them saying, "David Bowie is in the club. If you come around we'll introduce you."

I couldn't believe it because, you know, although I already had a letter from him, I'd never met him, and he was really at the apex of his coolness and fame. So I quickly got dressed up and went round. The weird thing about meeting Bowie is like people say when they met the Queen – they can't remember what she said.

TOM ROBINSON

When I first came to London I looked in the back of *Time Out* and it had listings that included gay pubs. When I walked into my first gay pub I thought I'd died and gone to heaven. Soon afterwards I went to a Gay Liberation Front disco in Kings Cross and got picked up by a young British Rail guard who took me back to his flat and I spent the night with him.

When I came downstairs in the morning there was a record playing in his living room where he'd set out the breakfast stuff and he had a log fire blazing in the grate. As I walked in the door, on came a David Bowie record, "Wake up you sleepy head, put on some clothes, shake up your bed, put another log on the fire for me, I've made some breakfast and coffee, looked out my window what do I see? A crack in the sky and a hand reaching down to me."

It was just serendipitous that I came into the room at the moment he'd just put that album on and that song was playing. It was like the soundtrack of my life.

It was the first time in all those years as a music fan that I'd heard a song about me. All through the Sixties even the gay artists changed the genders so a song like Lennon's 'You've Got to Hide Your Love Away,' which was clearly about Brian Epstein, still said, "If she's gone I can't go on."

I'd listened to that as a teenage music fan and thought, that sounds almost like what I'm feeling. But with Bowie it actually *was* what I was feeling. We could all, our generation of queer kids, read into Bowie's music whatever we wanted. His message was diluted and very ambiguous and as a result he was able to get it all the way around the world and into the bedrooms of lonely isolated teenagers in every country. When I formed my band and wrote 'Glad to be Gay' I learned from that.

PETER TATCHELL

Tom Robinson's Seventies hit song 'Glad to be Gay' was the queer national anthem. It was such a positive affirmation of our right to be and such a damning indictment of the homophobia we faced. We sang that with such pride and such gusto. For us it really meant something to have that song by a gay man for our community.

TOM ROBINSON

In the gay clubs, in the safety of these kind of protected spaces in London where the metropolitan elite were getting their kicks and having their dances and stuff. These badges that said 'Glad to be Gay' started appearing and people started wearing them on the dance floor. But then as they left the club they'd take them off so they didn't get attacked or beaten up in the street.

MARC ALMOND

I never think Tom Robinson gets the credit that he really deserves, because he was really the first person I can remember coming out and saying, "I'm glad to be gay."

That statement. Not just, "I'm gay." But "I'm glad to be gay." Before then, gay people all had to be miserable.

It wasn't just an expression of gayness, it was an expression of freedom, freedom to break down those barriers.

TOM ROBINSON

I had always been a fan of music and my dad had forced me to play the piano until I was 13. When I was at Finchden Manor one of the old boys came down – the broadcaster and blues man Alexis Corner. There were about 40 of us boys crammed in the room. He casually took out an acoustic guitar and sang without embarrassment in this room full of strangers about corrupt policemen, racism, poverty, heartbreak, the whole panoply of the blues, Muddy Waters, Curtis Mayfield and his own songs – it was a revelation. So Alexis was a great role model for me and he mentored my first band, which I formed when I moved to London.

I suppose the fact I'd worked with a New York group called Hot Peaches who were doing an eyewitness account of the Stonewall riot made me feel that bit more militant. Added to that the fact that I'd seen the Sex Pistols, and that punk was starting to happen. It was clear that something was going to erupt and that you kind of had to nail your colours to the mast. All of that led me to write a song called 'Sing if you're glad to be gay' as a sarcastic comment. It listed all the bad things that were happening, then said, so try and sing if you're glad to be gay with all that going on. It was a furious song.

I decided to form a band of my own and go and play gigs in pubs. 'Glad to be Gay' was a kind of confrontation with the audience in the way that punk was about. Bizarrely, we didn't get bottled off the stage and people actually went "Yeah! fair enough."

So really, we got lucky.

JON SAVAGE

Punk was a movement of the outsider, the weirdo, the disaffected. There was a whole contingent of early punk fans called the *Bromley Contingent* and there were people around them who were gay or bisexual.

It initially began like that, but then when the music industry got involved punk became four-man macho rock and roll. I always thought it was completely ridiculous that people can be macho in punk because of its original slang meaning, which was the young man who took it up the bum in prison. So how can you be macho and be a punk?

It took Tom Robinson to really take up the cudgel. With 'Glad to be Gay' he wasn't so much playing punk as benefitting from the space punk had opened up.

MARC ALMOND

You could sing that song even if you weren't gay, but just in solidarity with somebody, being able to express their freedom. It was a great expression of that and I felt he was really the first person to do it.

JON SAVAGE

I believe music is ahead of politics; it's always ahead of politics. Music is very sophisticated, it's very immediate, it hits the body, it hits the mind, it hits the heart. So it's very powerful when it works. I really do believe that the pop music of the Seventies and Eighties helped people come to terms with homosexuality.

TOM ROBINSON

Once the *Tom Robinson Band* had started going out and gigging, *London Weekend Television* approached us and said, "We're doing this program about young gay people in London. We'd like you to come on and sing your 'Glad to be Gay' song."

I consulted with my manger friend at the time and he said, "You know what, we don't want to just end up as a one issue band, a one song band."

So we cheekily said back to Janet Street Porter, "We'll only come on and do 'Glad to be Gay' if you'll also let us do this other song called '2468 Motorway'."

So they let us do that and once we'd been on the telly things really escalated.

'2468 Motorway' was the obvious song to have come with first – just to establish our credentials as a band and build an audience on whom we could then unload an EP that contained 'Glad to be Gay'. I think if we'd gone straight in with 'Glad to be Gay' we'd have had a limited audience and struggled to get regular rock and punk fans to listen to the band at the time.

MATTHEW PARRIS

Tom Robinson's song, 'Glad to be Gay' meant a huge amount to me. I actually went to the Fairfield Halls in Croydon to watch him and felt very brave. It would seem quite tame now, but it didn't at the time.

LORD SMITH

While I was not yet publicly out, I'd completely accepted it in myself – I was gay and I was going to enjoy it. This was helped by popular culture, like Tom Robinson singing 'Glad to be Gay'. But it wasn't just those sort of things, it was also that, gradually (and this happened very gradually), people in all walks of life began to be more open about who and what they were. It helped even more than public figures coming out when people you knew, who you counted as friends and were part of your community, began saying, "Yeah, I happen to be gay."

CHAPTER FIVE

Reaping the rewards

TOM ROBINSON

In that pre-internet age it was wonderful to walk into my first gay pub and see a man selling *Gay News*. Instead of just one listing at the back of *Time Out*, I now had a whole newspaper. It came out every two weeks – a whole social world with people openly hugging each other in clubs and being unashamed to have their faces published in a national newspaper. *Gay News* covered lesbian events as well as gay men's events and bisexual events and what have you. It was not discriminatory it was all inclusive.

PETER TATCHELL

Gay Liberation Front activists set up the collective that established Britain's first gay community newspaper, *Gay News*. A very important stepping stone because it was through *Gay News* that LGBT people around the country were connected and informed. *Gay News* played an incredibly important role in cementing LGBT identity and community and give us a sense of focus on the battle for equal rights. It exposed homophobia, it reported on challenges to it. *Gay News* was a real milestone.

TOM ROBINSON

I discovered I could buy *Gay News* from a news stand on my way to work. To me that was much more important than buying it from a seller in a gay pub. The total message of gay liberation was that you've got to live openly, and I honestly believe that's how we've come as far as we have in this time – it's because of individual people living openly and coming out to their friends, families and work mates.

As a first step in that I decided to read my *Gay News* on the tube in a crowded train and I opened it up, fully expecting somebody to challenge me. Sure enough, over my left shoulder there was this presence – a pin-striped presence looming over me, who I could just tell was dying to say something. He was just clearing his throat, bowler hat, brief case and I could only see him in my peripheral vision, but I knew he was itching to say something and so, finally, just before I got to my stop he cleared his throat and said: "The fortnights seem to fly by don't they?"

It was fantastic. It was wonderful. It was a great moment.

PETER TATCHELL

For me the Gay Liberation Front was beyond just gay rights. It was a movement for LGBT people and also a movement for social liberation. In the Gay Liberation Front the word equality never passed our lips, we were interested in something much bigger. We didn't want equality within the *status quo* that we were critical of, we wanted to transform society to benefit everyone, LGBT and straight. So our agenda was very much about lining up with the women's liberation movement, the black liberation movement, the Irish freedom struggle, and the battles of working class people in trade unions. We saw ourselves as a revolutionary movement to hopefully bring about a better society for everyone

JON SAVAGE

The Campaign for Homosexual Equality was a serious movement in the UK. It did a lot of lobbying work and was partly responsible for getting the law changed in 1967, but that was a world away from pop music. You can change the law, but you've got to change public attitudes too, and public attitudes were certainly informed by pop music.

I regard politicos as being a separate beast from pop fans. I think to do that political work, to do that lobbying work, to do those demonstrations, you're not a pop person. There's a limit to how much the two worlds can mix because they're so different.

STEPHEN K. AMOS

When I think about growing up in London in the Seventies we had one big deal. People who, like me, had parents either from Africa or the Caribbean, had the race issue. We had no time to think about anything else because the one thing you cannot hide is your race, your ethnicity. You can't hide it, but you can hide your sexuality, or your sexual orientation. And you know, back in the day, because I wasn't quite sure what I was, and saw nothing and no one who looked like me who I could identify with, it was much easier to say nothing.

For me it would have needed seeing a role model, a black and out proud man who sounded like me or my father, someone who wasn't particularly camp and wasn't a hairdresser – and I didn't see that.

MARC ALMOND

I didn't really become aware of myself as a gay person until the beginning of the Eighties, which is when I think I experienced the worst homophobia, not just boys at school calling you a poof and things like that but when I began to be well known I suddenly started to get this hatred back, really open homophobic nastiness. I felt I was in this different kind of school playground at the beginning of the Eighties and it was quite a disturbing time for me. It probably sent me off the rails even more than my parents breaking up.

STEPHEN K. AMOS

My mum loved Danny La Rue, Larry Grayson, Russell Harty – all those really famous TV personalities. At that time none of them had acknowledged publicly they were gay, it was just part of their natural persona. The thought that they might have been gay didn't even cross my mum's mind. Homosexuality wasn't a subject that was discussed in the family.

MATTHEW PARRIS

There's an awful lot of nostalgia about the old gay scene, about the ghetto, as it were, and about how we had our own language, and it was all great fun, and we were all members of a slightly secret society. But I don't buy it. It was a bit of fun for some people but I found all the gay language a bit stupid.

I didn't want to be camp, I wasn't naturally a camp person, and I didn't suppose that being a gay person meant you were camp, or effeminate, or limp-wristed, or like Larry Grayson, or used funny language. I felt that confined people and tied them down and was rather self-oppressive, as if you felt you had to conform to a certain type of stereotype if you wanted to be gay.

SIMON CALLOW

I concluded then, which I maintain and have always maintained, that despite occasional nasty setbacks, essentially British people rather like their gays, they like us, they just find us entertaining and colourful and sort of talented as well as different and unusual.

LORD BROWNE

In 1971, there was a movie, *Sunday Bloody Sunday*. I was in New York at the time and I saw it in a very small movie house – because it was regarded as dangerous, or non-appropriate, or not very commercial. It was remarkable to make such a movie, remarkable. Especially with the actors, the stars, it had in it.

STEPHEN FRY

I didn't see *Sunday Bloody Sunday* till I was older but what I did see was a film magazine with a picture of a kiss between Peter Finch and Murray Head. Yeah, just a kiss, a photograph of a kiss in a film magazine. But to know there was a film out there with that kiss in it, it just sent shivers down the spine, it was extraordinary. The director of the film, John Schlesinger, and that generation of film makers, you know they made quite a difference, like Jack Gold who directed *The Naked Civil Servant*.

PETER TATCHELL

The Naked Civil Servant was a real breakthrough in terms of public entertainment and visibility for LGBT issues. It was an incredibly moving and powerful film and I think for people who identified as trans it was also significant. The public reaction was really interesting and surprising. Overwhelmingly the reaction was positive and the film elicited sympathy and I think even Quentin Crisp's critics couldn't detract from the fact that the life he lived was incredibly brave and courageous. I think it presented gay people in a very different way – not as victims but as defiant, and that was a really important signal.

STEPHEN FRY

What was remarkable about *The Naked Civil Servant* was that I didn't really think it as being about a gay man. It was about a unique individual because Quentin Crisp and I shared absolutely nothing in terms of our style, and his style was far greater than mine would ever be. His style was a piece of performance art. It was his courage and his strength that John Hurt managed to convey as much as anything. The way he could walk with his head held high, his hair purple and pink, dressed with those rather frothy scarfs and cute lapels, looking obviously like an effeminate homosexual, which is how he described himself.

TRIS PENNA

I thought John Hurt playing that role was amazing, and of

course at school the next day the name 'Quentin' suddenly became a new term of abuse and I was called it a few times. You know children, teenagers, "Oh, *Quen*-tin!"

I thought it was empowering seeing John Hurt walking down the street and at that point I probably would have dyed my own hair orange. It was like, "Fuck off everybody."

I quite like that 'we're queer and we're here' sort of in-your-face stuff. I definitely like confrontation

MARC ALMOND

When the public became aware of me, I suddenly started to get this hatred. When I walked down the street people would shout out the window, things like that.

One great thing about growing up during that time, it gave me the armour to deal with all that kind of crap. The stuff that really scared me though, came from the media. The insidious comments about me, and also the homophobia I experienced on television, comedians taking the micky out of you in a very kind of fay, camp, effeminate way. I was watching *Jukebox Jury* one night, when it was hosted by Jools Holland. One of the artists on the program played one of my records and did this terrible, offensive, mincing impression of me. I didn't recognise myself at all, but it still hurt. Really wounded me, more than I'd ever been hurt in the school playground.

JON SAVAGE

Marc Almond, and his group Soft Cell, were very important. They were huge and they were very obviously deviant. They were brilliant, they were touching, and they were emotional. Marc was so wonderful when he came on *Top of the Pops*, with all the Nancy Cunard bracelets going up his arm and, you know, doing all the movements. They had this wonderful string of hits that lasted for two or three years and really paved the way for so many people, like Steve Strange and Boy George and the *Blitz* club.

MARK WARDEL

Blitz was incredible. It was full of very ambitious mostly gay people who were fiercely protective of their individuality. Everyone was following this David Bowie ethos of self-reinvention. All the gay people at the *Blitz*, like Boy George and Steve Strange, what they were doing was inventing an exaggerated persona and name. They were assuming these artificial personas in which they could live their life slightly outside of the mainstream. The *Blitz* was full of very ambitious people who were very creative and competitive so the air was thick with hairspray fumes and feuds because people would fall out for years over who had copied a certain person's hair style. For instance, the first time I saw Boy George he had two-foot high hair with stuffed parrots in it. And the makeup was just beyond.

WILL YOUNG

Boy George was like a life line really, it was someone who was public, and gay, and themselves.

STEVE BLAME

Boy George used to always say he preferred a cup of tea to sex, and then a bit later he would say he preferred coffee. He was putting up a front to appear to be the non-sexual acceptable homosexual of that time. It was much more acceptable to be gay if you weren't considered a sexual character, you had to be sort of anodyne. He was more like a painted doll.

JON SAVAGE

So there was this whole wave of what was rather quaintly called gender-bending, and it worked both ways. You had

Grace Jones and Annie Lennox posing like men, and you had Boy George. It was like a re-run of glam rock only better because it was hilarious, with them all sniping and bitching about each other. And then out of that gender-bending moment came Bronski Beat and Jimmy Somerville.

MARC ALMOND

David Bowie and Marc Bolan had opened a door for me but Jimmy Somerville went somewhere altogether new. He was brave. He didn't go out there with makeup or a gender confusing image, he went out as a regular young guy, but a gay guy. His videos had no kind of pretence of anything else but being gay. He just said, "I am a gay person. I'm gay right from the word go."

He presented himself in a checked shirt and jeans and a crewcut. In other words, "I look just like regular kind of guy who goes out to regular clubs or whatever." But his videos were quite clearly of young men loving other young men.

JON SAVAGE

Jimmy Somerville looked like somebody who went to the Dog and Whistle. There was that whole kind of early Eighties flannel shirt business that was very big in the gay world. But he didn't act gay, he wasn't dressing up, he wasn't doing a Marc Almond. He looked straight. And of course, that's every straight man's biggest fear – if I can't tell whether they're gay or not, could I be gay myself?

MATT LUCAS

People say that gay people are promiscuous, but I don't think it's gay people who are promiscuous, I think it's men. Men like to have sex, and I think men are generally more capable of having loveless sex and enjoying it, and separating those two emotions of love and lust, than women are. So when people say gay men are promiscuous, I think if straight men had sex with each other they would be just as promiscuous. It's about men, because men are dogs.

TRIS PENNA

Around then, there was a very dark period. It coincided with a resurgence of heavy drug taking on the gay scene. I went to a club where Lee Barry was performing, for example, and when you went to the toilet for a wee there were bloody syringes on the floor. People were into heroin, that was the big drug, and that was when Holly Johnson arrived on the scene with *Frankie Goes to Hollywood* and 'Relax'.

MARC ALMOND

And then of course came the dreaded holocaust of AIDS, which gave everyone an excuse to hate gay people even more.

CHAPTER

SIX

An unwanted visitor

SIMON CALLOW

AIDS was the sudden knee in the groin because something had been happening. The summers of love had turned into something a little bit more driven and obsessive. Gay men began to think that having sex was a duty. If you hadn't had sex on any one day then you had failed in life, and preferably sex two or three or four times with two or three or four different people. I wasn't untouched by that obsessiveness. But I drew right back from it because I knew that you ceased to live your own life. I started to pull back – but you did feel there was a madness going on.

My friend Martin Showman called New York "Babylon on the Hudson." But here in London it was "Babylon on The Thames." I mean there was a sort of frenzy going on and somehow it erupted into AIDS. I'm not saying even that it was caused by it, by any means. It was a phenomenon that sprang up in our midst with the most terrifying intensity at a moment when it looked as though the party was getting out of control. Suddenly we were all arrested in the most terrifying way and that was the great defining moment of modern homosexuality.

STEPHEN FRY

It's timing was extraordinary. It seemed, you know, almost you could believe some of the wild preachers in America who claimed it was 'God's punishment' because it came at the very sort of crest of the reaping of the rewards of the early Gay Liberation movement.

TOM ROBINSON

First thing I remember hearing about AIDS was that Elton John said to me, "Have you heard about this thing in America where there's some disease that's killing gay men in San Francisco."

I said, "No, what is it?"

He said, "Well I don't know but apparently it's happening."

PAUL GAMBACCINI

Of course, the gay capitals of America proceeded Britain. I remember being in New York in 1983 and returning to a still sleeping London and saying to my housemate. "There's a new disease and no one knows what's causing it. From now on fucking is banned in this house."

We went to Heaven and stood on the landing. I looked down and said, "A quarter of these people are going to die and they don't know it yet."

That was slightly conservative. I think a third of them probably died within a few months.

TRIS PENNA

It wasn't until the mid-Eighties that you knew anything about it, it was just lots of people in America dying and lots of people older than me dying. Then suddenly it was people who I knew who were dying, and young people too. I'll be honest with you, we were convinced we were all going to die.

TOM ROBINSON

The rumors continued to spread and then you heard of the first deaths in London. People said if you take poppers that's what's causing it, because all the men that died had used poppers extensively.

TRIS PENNA

At this point nobody knew what it was. Was it because you sniffed poppers? Was it because you kissed? Was it because of this, was it because of that? I can remember being paranoid that if I even kissed somebody I was going to catch it. We didn't know. It was like the plague, a plague that only affected gay people – gay men and black people. There wasn't that much sympathy for anyone.

PAUL GAMBACCINI

A nation's response to HIV depended on which communities were first affected. In Belgium it was black Africans because of the association with the former Belgium Congo. In Japan it was a disease of foreigners. Whoever had it first was stigmatised first. In New York, where it hit before London, it was the so-called *Four H Club*: homosexuals, hemophiliacs, heroin users and Haitians (because Haiti appears to have been a way station in the geographical spread from Africa). Those four groups were discriminated against because they were the first to be infected, so in that sense it wasn't preordained there would be increased anti-gay prejudice, it was just that gay people were in the forefront.

JON SAVAGE

The problem with AIDS when it hit was that it was also accompanied by a tabloid backlash and there was a lot of victim blaming. In particular, the Murdoch press behaved completely disgracefully and so suddenly a lot of the gains which had been made were in danger of being wiped out, and it was a very bad thing to be gay again.

TOM ROBINSON

People started dying long before we knew what the disease was, or how it was transmitted. I lost so many friends and lovers, dear wonderful people in the Eighties. They didn't know what was causing it, they didn't know how to protect themselves and there was no way of saving them.

TRIS PENNA

There was certainly a feeling amongst the public that there

was some kind of gay holocaust going on and that gay people themselves were in some way to blame for it.

THE REVEREND FORESHEW-CAIN

At the local church when I was at University there was a post board outside that said, "Aids is the wrath of God."

Among conservative evangelicals there are people who still think that.

JON SAVAGE

Gays were being vilified in the press. A lot of people including myself were sure we'd got AIDS. Nobody knew that much about it, there was no cure, and people were dying in the most horrible way.

PAUL GAMBACCINI

To begin with the disease had a name that didn't last, GRID: *Gay Related Immune Deficiency*. Then came AIDS: *Acquired Immune Deficiency Syndrome*, which stuck. But AIDS was only the condition, not the actual disease. The actual disease was HIV: *Human Immunodeficiency Virus*.

LORD BROWNE

My only gay friend died of AIDS. I remember the chilling effect, the hugely chilling effect that it had on society in general. Actually, I didn't know he had died of AIDS until many years later. We just lost contact, and that was the tragedy of it.

JON SAVAGE

One of the big problems for gay people has always been rejection. Rejection by peers, particularly rejection by your family, and that came up very strongly in the Eighties. A lot of the people I knew who got AIDS then had the experience of being rejected by their family.

LORD CASHMAN

In the Eighties, with the hysteria and misrepresentation

of AIDS and HIV, it was a very difficult time for people to come out.

PAUL GAMBACCINI

I was visiting my best friend from college when a group of his friends come up to him and said, "I guess we'll see you Wednesday"

"Wednesday?" he asked.

"Yes," they said, "George's funeral."

He had no idea George had been ill. He asked me to excuse him for a moment and he stooped on the side of the street to weep, telling me George was the man he loved most in the Seventies. At the time I thought he was weeping for George. In retrospect I realised he was crying for himself because he knew he would die. And he did.

THE REVEREND ANDREW FORESHEW-CAIN

Recently, I watched a film, *Longtime Companion*, about the AIDS crisis on the West Coast in the Eighties. It was at the time when I myself was becoming sexually aware and active, and AIDS was becoming very apparent, and it took me three days to watch that film. I found myself holding a tea towel, weeping, as I watched these young people who were dying. There's a moment in it when this beautiful young man who'd been so full of life, enjoying the freedoms that the early Eighties had begun to give gay people, suddenly wakes up in a hospital bed covered in Kaposi sarcoma, almost unable to breath, with fear in his eyes. I mean, I had to turn it off, I couldn't carry on.

STEVE BLAME

When AIDS came along the first thing I did, as soon as you could, was to go and have an AIDS test and I got AIDS paranoia, you know, I would buy a new pair of shoes and I'd get yellow marks on my feet from the shoes and I'd go to my best friend Anna, show her my feet and say, "I've got AIDS."

And she would go, "Don't be so fucking stupid."

One time when I went to get a blood test they said to me, "You know you have to have sex, don't you?"

I hadn't had sex between the last AIDS test and this one but I had this AIDS paranoia because a lot of people I knew had either contracted HIV or had actually died. I think a lot of people had that.

MATTHEW PARRIS

I was as worried as everybody else was about HIV. I imagine if assisted dying had been allowed in those days, there would be quite a few people who would have simply taken their own lives. I was prey, as everybody was, to the sudden terror that I had contracted the virus.

Like so many other people, I went along to a kind of hole-in-the-wall clinic, where you didn't have to give your name. Then it was too weeks till one got the results, and I remember those were two weeks in which I began to persuade myself that I must be HIV positive. I worked out how I was going to take my own life when I got the diagnosis, which I didn't. It was an intense time.

STEVE BLAME

When I started at MTV we had this show called *Reverb*, which was sort of reviewing the week's creativity and stuff. I said, "Let's get someone in who's got AIDS."

The guy we got had full-blown AIDS and we did an interview with him that was amazingly moving as it was still before any medication had been developed. He knew he was going to die and we did the interview with him live on air. When he left someone asked me, "Where did he sit?"

I pointed, and the person refused to sit where the guy had

been. It shocked me totally because I thought, "What is this? This is absolute insanity."

LORD CASHMAN

We must never forget those who should have known better, like the media and the tabloids who represented HIV as the 'gay plague'. They said you could catch it by picking up a cup, or a mug, or a beer glass that a gay man had used. Whether the gay man was HIV positive or not was irrelevant. So there was scaremongering and appalling discrimination against people who were living with HIV or groups who were likely to be HIV positive.

STEVE BLAME

There was a wave of hatred towards gay people but AIDS worked in two ways. It was a devastating and terrible disease. But with so many people dying of it more and more families began to find out there was someone in their extended family who had it. People began to realise that almost every family had a gay member and I think eventually that had an effect on people becoming more liberal.

LEE TRACEY

You would go to work and look at someone and know they'd got AIDS. I sat by the bedside of three of them when they were dying in a London hospital. Traumatic times. They called it the gay plague and it was the most horrendously horrific thing to see your friends laying there dying of this terrible, terrible disease. I went to too many funerals, most of us did, and many of the friends who succumbed did so simply because they wouldn't take precautions. I never understood why gay people would go and have sex with somebody they didn't even know and not wear something. I used to tell people, "If you want to have sex with somebody, male or female, wear something."

Sometimes it was like talking to a brick wall.

MATTHEW PARRIS

There was a fairly widespread understanding among gay people as to where the big risks were. I think if I had been better looking I would be dead now, because I would have slept with a lot more people. The best protection for me against contracting the HIV virus was that not too many people wanted to sleep with me. In retrospect, perhaps it saved my life

MARC ALMOND

People often say, "Weren't the Eighties great!" but they weren't for me. The whole ten years was actually quite a hellish time.

PAUL GAMBACCINI

I had the honour of being one of the people asked to participate in the first AIDS health awareness campaign. Another one was Ian Dury. He said, "I used to sing about sex and drugs and rock and roll. Now only one of them is safe."

CHAPTER

SEVEN

The AIDS Pandemic

SIMON CALLOW

This ghastly kind of parade went on and on and on. It went on for years. The funerals. The funerals one after the other. Oh, unbearable. And the visits to people in hospital. The helplessness of it all.

PETER TATCHELL

By then we had a blanket ban on gay and bisexual men donating blood for their entire lifetime.

PAUL GAMBACCINI

We were as backs-against-the-wall as anyone could be, we were dying, and there were a lot of people in authority saying, "It's good that you're dying".

SIMON CALLOW

And in the face of all that, how the fuck could you care about whether people knew you were gay or not? You were just going to go in and help.

PAUL GAMBACCINI

You had to engage with it, you had to fight it, you just had to do your best.

SIMON CALLOW

It was of course a period of terror for many of us and it was just a lottery. Some people drew the short straw and some of us were miraculously spared having done exactly the same thing as everybody else. Governments, for the most part, were incapable of dealing with something like AIDS, so people took things into their own hands and started creating organisations to help each other, and some wonderful things came out of it, like London Lighthouse, which revolutionised treatment for terminal illnesses.

MATTHEW TODD

Princess Diana started going to AIDS hospices and shaking

hands with people with HIV. It was an incredible thing, another light in the darkness. No one had ever done that before and she got abuse from MPs and journalists for doing it. People with AIDS were considered to be like vermin in the press and for her to do that and make a speech about people with AIDS needing a hug, it was absolutely incredible.

PETER TATCHELL

The Terrence Higgins Trust spearheaded the fight against HIV. It provided the only effective HIV education and the only effective support for people with the virus. It wasn't until the first heterosexual people began dying from HIV that the government began to sit up and act.

MATTHEW PARRIS

It was the health minister Norman Fowler who took the personal initiative to do something. I don't think he was under huge pressure from his civil servants, and he certainly wouldn't have been under pressure from the prime minister. It wasn't the kind of thing she got involved with. But Norman decided this mattered and the government could make a difference; the government had to be on the side of gay people rather than just be seen to warn and persecute

LORD SMITH

Norman Fowler was really good in taking it seriously, fighting for the resources and making sure the money went in the right direction.

PAUL GAMBACCINI

He managed to convince the prime minister, Margaret Thatcher, though she was rolling her eyelids a bit, and we had the health information campaign that peeked famously with the John Hurt iceberg TV commercial.

PETER TATCHELL

The great AIDS tombstone advertising campaign in the press and on TV. It was shock horror and it played to the tabloid narrative of a 'gay plague'. It created a climate of fear. Too much fear, I think, and not enough facts and education.

LORD CASHMAN

And into that mix, the BBC introduced into *Eastenders*, the most successful show on television, these two gay characters. They were ordinary men and they normalised homosexuality. There were questions in parliament as to why, with AIDS and HIV spreading around the country, a gay character was allowed in a family show. The courage of the of the BBC in advancing that storyline did a great deal to change public opinion.

MATT LUCAS

Seeing the characters of Colin and Barry in *EastEnders* was really important. To have those people there, as much as anything, was about viability.

LORD CASHMAN

It was on the front page of *The Sun* when I went into *EastEnders*, they outed my partner to his family in the *News of the World* with the centre pages, "Secret Gay Love of AIDS Scare East Ender," mixing up the fact that I lived in the East End and I was in *EastEnders*, and that there was an AIDS story in the show. They printed our address and that afternoon a brick came through the window. Do you back off because that happens? Strangely enough, it makes you stronger, because you don't want to let the bastards win.

TRIS PENNA

Shortly after that was the time when the first drugs started to become available and there was a little glimmer of hope.

PAUL GAMBACCINI

I lost so many friends and lovers, dear wonderful people in the Eighties. These were young men who were handsome and intelligent, with their whole lives ahead of them, several of my closest friends. I did some volunteer work, driving for The *Terence Higgins Trust*. I was only peripherally involved but it led me to be very self-righteous about condoms, and it was using a condom that saved my life. My partner at the time turned out to be HIV positive and I was negative because we'd always used a condom. So in many ways I owe my life to the *Terence Higgins Trust*.

STEPHEN FRY

I would find myself sitting on the bed of a boy, a dear friend I'd been at university with who was looking skeletal, with dreadful waxy skin and Kaposi sarcoma and breathing difficulties, with all the hospital equipment of a dying person. And there are his parents with tear-filled eyes, and next to them is the boy's lover, who for some reason is not HIV positive. The parents have just discovered their son is gay and has got this disease they've been reading about. And they are thinking, "You did that to my boy."

Sometimes they couldn't cope and they'd cry and leave and maybe not even come back. That happened with one of the parents. The mother didn't come back to see her son – she was just too angry, too upset – couldn't process it. But one also saw parents who came in and when their son fell asleep, or had to go off, they would talk to the other men in the ward and they would go around and chat to them. And when their son died they would come back as visitors, and they changed utterly, they changed their outlook on the world.

SIMON CALLOW

Somehow, out of all that horror was summoned some kind of serenity, some kind of calm, some kind of peace. It was an extraordinary and deeply moving time and I don't know what the effect has been on gay life or on our sense of ourselves as homosexuals. But one thing I do know absolutely, it made people realise that being in the closet simply wasn't an option.

JULIAN CLARY

There were things going on that you couldn't make up. James Anderton, the Chief of Police in Manchester, said that gay people were "swirling in a human cesspit of their own making," and that AIDS was all our fault. I had a photograph of him that I brought on stage and I used to kiss it and sing to it, "Answer, answer my prayer. Please God strike him down."

And there were police raids on the Vauxhall Tavern with all these policemen wearing rubber gloves.

PAUL GAMBACCINI

Everywhere in the popular press you saw AIDS referred to as the 'gay plague'. Well do you want to know just how NON-gay a plague this was?

I was interviewed not long ago by a man who in 1983 was a student in a school for haemophiliac children. He was in a class of 50 kids where the blood transfusions they were given were contaminated. He was the only one who lived – 49 died. He was now trying to make sense of it all by interviewing other people about HIV. So that's how non-gay this was.

ELTON JOHN

During the years when AIDS started to happen and during the Eighties and the beginning of the Nineties I wasn't there. I got sober in 1990 and when I looked back on my life I thought I didn't do enough. I wasn't really at the heart of the anger which I should have been at. I'd lost so many friends I couldn't figure out why I'd been so absent from this kind of fight against AIDS. And obviously it was down to my addiction and my self-obsession.

PAUL GAMBACCINI

We lost so many of our dearest. And because we went to so many funerals and visited so many people in hospital, we didn't have time to grieve each individual with the time and thoughtfulness they deserved. It was just on to the next hospital bed.

Years later, when they come to mind, when their name is mentioned, you think – oh my God.

It hits you even harder than it did at the time because now we have the breathing space to consider all these lost lives.

STEPHEN FRY

During the AIDS epidemic of the Eighties one saw both the best and the worst of what humans can be. You saw glorious heroism and terrible cowardliness and cruelty. I left university in exactly the year HIV arrived in the Western world and plowed its deadly furrow through America, Britain, Europe and primarily Africa. During that time a lot of my friends had to tell their parents they were gay and in the same sentence tell them they were going to die very soon, and die one of the most horrible deaths that nature has yet devised.

MATTHEW TODD

AIDS and HIV has been so incredibly traumatic for gay and bisexual men that I think it's overwhelmed us. Sometimes we cannot bare to even think about it so we push the condom out the way. We don't talk about HIV and AIDS and we don't have an event or a memorial to the people we lost. Young people have no idea how bad it was and how utterly devastating the whole thing was and that worries me a lot.

STEVE BLAME

When AIDS first arrived, I was going to night clubs enjoying myself having sex with people and not thinking about it. Then suddenly those adverts arrived equating AIDS to death, and friends of mine died. I used to go to a club called Lazers in North London around 1982. Ten years later when I was working for MTV I did an interview with the Greek owner and I asked him, "Why did you shut the club?"

He told me, "Everyone died."

It was such a shocking thing to hear but it was true. Because in a night club situation like that, people were meeting each other every week and having sex.

PETER TATCHELL

At the World Summit of Ministers of Health for AIDS Prevention in 1988, we presented the world's first AIDS and HIV human rights charter. It changed the agenda from gore and panic to a final day declaration that pledged to protect people with HIV from persecution.

It was the first time any global body had done that and it marked the turning point away from repression and towards support and education.

JON SAVAGE

Out of that terrible situation with AIDS came all the lobbying and intense politicking of the late Eighties. It was a huge turnaround and it only happened because gay peoples' backs were up against the wall.

PETER TATCHELL

The night before the *World Health Summit* we held a huge candle-lit march from Hyde Park to the summit venue. To see the whole of Whitehall filled with thousands of people with candles was one of the most moving, incredible sights of my life. It was just so wonderful to see people take a stand against prejudice and discrimination and to affirm the human rights of people with HIV.

STEPHEN FRY

One of the good things that came out of AIDS was the way it spawned various organisations that have helped enormously on the journey since. Like the Terence Higgins Trust, which was named after the first person in Britain to die from AIDS. His friends got together to raise money to help other victims of the disease. And then Elton John formed the Elton John Foundation.

ELTON JOHN

It was a very defining moment for me personally when I set up the Elton John Foundation. I was determined that this should have a huge impact on my life.

STEPHEN FRY

I think at first Elton intended the foundation to be for people suffering closest at hand, in Britain and America, but it very rapidly became an obsession with Elton and his husband, David, to do what they could to highlight what was going on in sub-Saharan Africa, particularity with issues like mother to child transmission.

ELTON JOHN

I'm proud of what we've achieved, I'm proud of the money we've raised and the projects we've started. But we have so much further to go with stigma. Solving stigma is the biggest problem we have.

STEPHEN FRY

The stigma is just terrible – total pathological destruction – women giving birth to HIV positive babies is a disastrous outcome of the disease. The important thing is, when gay people see what's happening in their own relatively small community, it's very hard not to connect it to the wider world of disadvantaged marginalised people.

ELTON JOHN

I hate the fact that anyone is marginalised because of what colour their skin is, or what sexual orientation they are, or what they believe in. You have to go out in the field and see the response. Because if we just hear second hand we don't really get the impact. When you go over into the front, whether it's America, Ukraine, Africa, India, or wherever, and see what the money does, and see the gratitude on people's faces, that makes you even more prepared to go the extra mile.

STEPHEN FRY

I think it's simply wonderful that someone like Elton, an inspirational figure for many millions with his huge musical genius and all the ups and downs of his life, should create this enormous trust fund to put money into the world of AIDS relief.

ELTON JOHN (addressing the AIDS 2012 Convention in Washington DC)

"Because of their HIV status, because of their sexuality, because of their poverty, they feel marginalized and left out. Shame and stigma prevent them from getting help, from getting treatment. We have to replace the shame with love. We have to replace the stigma with compassion. No one should be left behind."

CHAPTER EIGHT

Coming out

JASON PRINCE

When I was 14, I was at a new school, my parents had moved a lot when I was a kid, and we moved to a new town called Crawley, near Gatwick airport. When I was first there I suffered a little bit of bullying for the first time in my life. Some of the more macho boys called me a few names and I thought – right, OK, this is going to be a little bit of a make or break for me.

But I loved drama and music and made really good friends with the drama teacher, and he said to me, "We're going to do a pop concert where everybody dresses up as their favourite pop star and sings their favourite pop song."

I was thinking – shall I be Wham! or Bros? But my favourite singer at the time was Sinitta. So, at the age of 14, I dressed up as her and sung 'Toy Boy' in assembly to show the other kids what they had to do.

After being in full drag at the age of 14, I don't think there was really any need to come out.

MARC ALMOND

I was bullied a bit at school, but it had its advantages – like other boys gravitating towards you who wanted to use you as a vehicle for their sexual experimentation, which you were only too willing to participate in. But, you didn't think of yourself as being gay, or homosexual, or things like that. You didn't have those labels put upon you then.

I left school at 17 and went to art college, which enabled me to find out the person I was. I felt my sexuality was still more fluid at that time and I didn't really put myself into a pigeon hole. I was able to use art college as a springboard for expressing myself freely.

ZOE LYONS

I think it began to dawn on me about the age of 11. Something was just starting to awaken and things began to drop into place, you know. It's that realisation when you're a kid that you're not going to be a part of the main group for a while, you're going to be a bit different, you're going to stick out a bit. And as a kid, I didn't want to stick out. I didn't want to be different.

WILL YOUNG

I first knew I was gay very early, I would say from about four or five. I remember watching *Dynasty* and fancying Bobby more than fancying Crystal. You know even at that age you get a sense of some sort of sexual feelings.

ZOE LYONS

I was never a girly girl. My room was decorated with pretty pictures of Chrissie Hynde and Grace Jones, I had two *Barbies* and eight *Action Men*. And if I'm brutally honest, the *Barbies* were just for the *Action Men* on their days off. I was a tomboy, a real tomboy.

MANJINDER SINGH SIDHU

I started going through puberty very early, at eight. And by 11 I knew I was gay.

I didn't really understand what it was because there was no evidence of it in the Indian society my family had brought me up in. So I got scared and kept the secret within me. But at school in Birmingham 98% of the kids were Asian and black and they called me gay boy, or batty boy. Children can see the difference and they point it out, so from the age of 18 I was out to everyone except my family. They couldn't see it and I couldn't tell them.

MATTHEW TODD

I came out during a Christian Union discussion at school with my friend, who was also gay. We plucked up courage and asked, "What do you think about gay people? What does Christianity think about gay people?"

The guy said, "Well we don't hate you but we think you need counselling."

We were completely outraged that he said we needed counselling, but ironically he was probably right. We *did* need counselling – not to do what he wanted, which was to stop being gay, but to help us accept being gay. I really needed that.

ZOE LYONS

When I was 15 or 16, I was looking for older people – examples in life – that I could can hang onto. But there wasn't an awful lot of positive imagery around.

WILL YOUNG

Having known about myself so early on didn't make it any easier to come to terms with. I had to live with the knowledge of what was coming – I wouldn't have kids, I wouldn't get married, that was a big thing. And the other big thing was I was a sinner, because I remember very clearly in divinity class talking about Sodom and Gomorrah and thinking that means men who fraternise with men.

I was very scared of being found out so I had a girlfriend. I was ashamed – yeah, shame – because you know shame is wrapped up with that sense of being different, the point of difference being fancying the same sex. It became very internally shameful.

OLLY ALEXANDER

It's a very complex and extremely powerful emotion, shame. When I was 16, I left my school and went to a performing arts college. I knew I was gay but I was still telling myself I could be straight if I wanted to be and until I moved to London, aged 18, I kept denying being gay. And of course, I felt shame, real shame.

STEVE BLAME

I felt I was completely alone as a young boy growing up, until that moment provided by David Bowie. Bowie helped me find a world that was out there that I felt that I belonged to. After that it was – fuck it, if this is who I am, so be it.

MANJINDER SINGH SIDHU

I'd been in Israel when I wrote and came out to my parents. My father ordered me back and I came back from hot Israel to the worst winter in the UK. I had no jacket and my family had been arguing and came late to the airport. I was standing out in the cold, shivering, I got in the car and they were just silent, there was no one talking. I didn't know what was going to happen. Was I going to be taken to an Indian doctor and made to take herbal medicine to try and change me? Was I going to be forced to marry a woman? Was I going to be kicked around and slapped? I didn't know.

MATTHEW TODD

I thought there was something about me that wasn't good enough so I needed to be better than everyone else, I needed to be a perfectionist. I would put my hand up first in class and always wanted to be answering the question, always wanted to be getting good marks from the teachers and would push myself forward. In school plays, if I didn't get the main part I'd be devastated and I'd go on like that the whole time, like I always had to be competitive. Maybe that's why there are so many famous and creative gays, compensating for being told they're not good enough. I had to be the best. I'd sit in school lessons obsessing about being famous. I'd think – I'm going to be in a limousine, I'm going to be spitting at all the people who were nasty to me, I'll show them, I'll show my parents. I will be amazing.

ZOE LYONS

I had feelings for a girl at school and I worried about it. I didn't want to be gay, I didn't want to be gay, I thought it might go away, and the advice was always, "Well it could always be just a phase, it's most likely a phase."

So I just kept thinking it will be a phase, and it will go away, and one day I'll suddenly wake up and desire a husband and live in Surrey.

LORD SMITH

I was certainly anxious. I'd never dreamed of talking with my parents about being gay, I only discovered it myself bit by bit. There were no norms in society, no role models you could look up to in those days, so it took a bit of getting used to. But once I'd completely accepted I was gay, even though I was not yet publicly out, I decided I was going to enjoy it. There were certain movies and television programs and music that helped to reinforce the sense that this was OK.

EVAN DAVIS

I was a happy homosexual in my early days, but I think it's important to say that in the Eighties, deep down, you were still aware it wasn't normal. You were aware that it wasn't the sort of, social thing – wasn't the thing that was done. We were in the world of, 'don't ask don't tell.' I was quite secretive about it, and very few people knew. I certainly didn't tell my parents.

DAN GILLESPIE SELLS

I always knew I was different, and when it came to the age of fancying boys, when I became kind of sexually aware and sexually active, all of that stuff, I struggled with being gay because I didn't want to be. Not because I thought there was anything wrong with it. I just didn't see that it was me.

MAJINDER SINGH SIDHU

My dad would ask things like, "Are you getting a feeling in the front or the back?" "What happens?" "Have you slept with anyone?" "Have you kissed a guy?": All these questions which I was mortified to answer. And then my mum would cry.

They took me to the local GP, who was a Sikh guy and traditional, but he was very nice. He told my dad, "This is how he's made and scientifically you can't change it."

So my dad took me to the local Sikh temple where they were also very nice. They said, "God created him like this and if he's going to change then only God can do it."

In the end my sisters helped my parents come to terms with it.

ZOE LYONS

My mum and dad had separated by the time I told them I was gay. I assumed my mum was a bit more hip than she actually was. She always told tales of seeing homosexuals in London in the Sixties on the Kings Road. She said you could always identify them because they wore a lot of velvet and big hats. So when I told her, I was quite surprised that she was so surprised. She took it in, then said. "It's a little bit like being told your child has got cancer."

In hindsight, that seems quite harsh, her choice of words could have been slightly better because it's *nothing* like being told your child has got cancer.

But I knew it wasn't going to be the end of our relationship. It wasn't silence and different rooms, I knew she always loved me, but it certainly took a long time for her to get over it. It was like watching someone have the wind knocked out of them and all she could think of was how hard and how difficult it was going to be for me.

BARONESS BARKER

When I went into the *House of Lords* I wasn't out, and I wasn't out for years afterwards. I remember saying to Paddy Ashdown when he asked me if I would go into the Lords, "I think there's a reason why you've asked me to do this. But I can't talk about that publicly."

He sat there, wise man that he was, and said, "No, you can't, not now, but you will at some stage and that will be fine."

LORD CASHMAN

In the Eighties, with the hysteria and misrepresentation of AIDS and HIV, it was a very difficult time for people to come out. But then Chris Smith, who was MP for Islington South and Finsbury, came out on a public platform and took our breath away. He was the first parliamentarian to come out, certainly the first parliamentarian in those aggressively homophobic, biphobic, transphobic years. He became a central figure in the new LGBT identity of *not* lying down and taking what society and the tabloids, and others who should know better, would throw at us. It was an incredible moment. Incredible.

LORD SMITH

One of the wonderful things for me personally was when I decided to come out publicly, in November 1984. The town of Rugby had got a new council in place and they'd decided they were going to remove sexual orientation from the list of things they were not going to discriminate about. So effectively they were saying they didn't want gay people working there.

There was a big protest march and because I'd said positive things about lesbian and gay rights, they asked me to go up and speak. I can remember sitting on the train preparing a very boring speech and it was only when I walked into the hall that I suddenly thought, now's the time to say something. Then it was my turn to speak, and I stood up and said, "My name is Chris Smith, I'm the Labour MP for Islington South and Finsbury, and I'm gay."

At that point the entire hall got to its feet and gave me a standing ovation. It's the only time I've ever had a standing ovation just one minute into a speech.

ANGELA EAGLE

For me coming out wasn't difficult. I always accepted what I was but I didn't talk about it a lot, I wasn't out when I first got elected though I wasn't hiding the fact. But I wanted to move in with my girlfriend and knew that I'd have to come out at some stage. So when we went into government I thought – well, I want to move in with my girlfriend and I'm a government minister, I need to make a positive statement about being a lesbian.

I talked first to my boss, John Prescott, the deputy prime minister. But trying to get in to see the deputy prime minister when you're one of his junior ministers without telling the civil service what you want to see him about is quite hard. They were going, "What's it about?"

"I just want to talk to him."

"But what's it about?"

"I just want to have a word with him."

Anyway, I went in to see him and I told him I was going to come out and that I was gay. He said, "Tell me something I didn't know already, love," then asked if he could give me a hug, to which I said yes.

I made the front page of the *Daily Mail* – "Lesbian in House of Commons."

It should have said 'shock horror' underneath, but it didn't.

DAN GILLESPIE SELLS

My dad lived separately. My two mums lived together and shared custody of me.

It was my mum's partner who forced me to come out. I didn't want to, I hadn't had a sexual experience, I didn't have a boyfriend, nothing had happened.

Although I knew I was gay, up until then it was just fantasies, and nobody wants to talk about sexual fantasies with their parents. If you have gay parents, it's amazing, it's great, it's like this wonderful thing where you know that whatever you choose is going to be great. But you still don't want to talk about it. Who wants to talk about sex with their parents?

So I was in this charity shop with my other mum and I picked out some particularity camp Seventies porcelain and said, "Oh, look at these, they're great,"

She probably looked at them and thought – that's the gayest thing I've ever seen. And she said, "Oh my God, just tell me, are you gay?"

I was like, "Yes, I'm gay." And that was it. Over.

BARONESS BARKER

After my mum died I knew I was going to come out publicly. I sat and thought for a long time and decided I had to do it in a way that had an impact, not just for me but for other people. So I did it during the second reading of the act on same sex marriage.

It's very strange, it's a speech that to this day people come up to me and thank me for doing. I don't see why they should thank me, I was just doing my job, but it clearly had a big impact on them. I understand people still watch it on YouTube.

One of the things I wasn't prepared for was to find out that my friends and colleagues had been concerned for me all along and worried about me being outed. Then when I came out it wasn't just a tremendous weight off my shoulders it was also a relief to the people who cared about me. I hadn't fully understood that until that moment.

QBOY

At school I knew I was gay. I started messing around with boys when I was very young so I was aware of that. But having everyone know you're gay and tell you you're gay when you haven't come out yourself is a really horrible experience. I really felt for Tom Daley when he was in a similar situation before he came out. Everybody was talking about it yet he hadn't actually admitted it publicly, nor even possibly to himself. You've got to be ready on a personal level to deal with your own sexuality in your own time. To have the people in my school, in my peer group, telling me I was gay when I wasn't ready to deal with it was bad enough, but imagine how terrible it must be when you have the whole country doing it to you and you're in the media.

BARONESS BARKER

I'm very envious of people who were able to come out at a much earlier stage than I did. It's why I hope that in the future something that I did helps young people to come out at a very early stage and not to go through the same trauma. But I defend the right of every individual person to choose the time that's right for them to come out, and I think that's non-negotiable.

MARC ALMOND

A gay journalist came to my home to do an interview with me who I thought was being more homophobic than a homophobe. "Oh look at that Judy Garland record," he said.

He was saying you must be gay, you know, because you have this record in your record collection. And I rather lost it and said, "Fuck it, yeah, I'm gay, I'm a faggot, I'm gay, gay, gay, gay, gay, gay."

So that was it. After that, there was kind of no going back. I desperately did try to climb back into the closet a little bit but the door was locked by that time and it was too late. And I hated that journalist with a vengeance because he made me do that; he made me sort of blow my mystery, blow my cover, blow my everything else. Even though you had to be stupid if you didn't kind of see it, but I hated him because I thought as a gay journalist that was a kind of homophobia, him having to drag me out screaming. I can't bare people that force people to come out of the closet who don't feel ready too, or who don't really want to.

JON SAVAGE

I interviewed Marc in autumn 1981 and popped the question, "Are you gay?"

Marc was a bit flustered and said, "Oh, I don't really want to talk about it."

Then a friend heard about it and pulled me up on it. "Jon, would you like to be asked that?"

I thought about it and – well, no, I wouldn't. I actually felt very sorry I'd put Marc on the spot. It wasn't really my job to do that.

MARK McADAM

Growing up I hated being gay and took every opportunity to

put it in a box and leave it separate from who I was. I didn't accept or understand who I was. I went to my first gay club at 19 and I spent the whole time worrying that someone would see me in there, and go, "Oh, that's that guy who does the media, that's the guy off the telly."

I could never be comfortable in those environments and it was only really around my mid-twenties, when I started to accept who I was and feel comfortable with myself, that I could.

There weren't any role models to look up to, or anyone to make you feel comfortable about yourself. I couldn't find anyone who I could say about – well I'm similar to that person, and look what he or she's doing, that's going to help me be accepting of myself.

I felt so ashamed of being gay that it was something that never really came into my life. I just took every opportunity to put it out of the way.

MAJINDER SINGH SIDHU

At university in London I did come into contact with a gay community and the gay scene, but it was predominantly white. I used to go to *Heaven* on a Wednesday and a Saturday and I was usually the only Asian guy there. There were some black guys there but there weren't any Asians. Anyway, I didn't actually want to hang out with Asian people because I felt like my community and my culture was backward and that they were homophobic. So I didn't have Asian friends, I had white friends, I wanted to be white, I wanted to be a coconut.

EVAN DAVIS

I can remember listening to Andy Bell of *Eurasia* being interviewed on the radio and he referred to his boyfriend, and there was no, kind of, deep intake of breath. He said, "My boyfriend and I are doing blah, blah, blah."

It made me realise that was the goal. That you could just talk about it like that without it being a big deal. My advice to people now when they talk about coming out is don't do the 'hey everyone gather round I've got something to tell you' thing. It's just too painful.

Just talk about it like they already know. Be completely unembarrassed about it. "Oh, my boyfriend and I just saw the new James Bond movie." And they'll be completely cool about it.

ANGELA EAGLE

I think the younger generation today just don't see what all the fuss is about, which is fantastic. Older generations have maybe got used to a particular way of being and it's not a very comfortable thing to sort of go into a room and go, "Oh, by the way I'm gay!" apropos of nothing. I mean heterosexual people don't have to come out. Also, there are all kinds of reasons why particular individuals might not want to come out that we can't know about. Whether it's an issue in the family, whether it's ageing parents, I don't think it's for us to judge.

PAUL GAMBACCINI

In 1971 while I was still a student at Oxford I did a cover story for *Rolling Stone* on Elton John, so I spent the day with Elton and Bernie Taupin. I felt a gust of freedom, because here was someone who was clearly openly gay though he wouldn't yet say so in the press, and he was giving me answers that for anyone who was gay made it obvious he was too. Like he was discussing someone who worked on the Cher show on American television and he said, "Better not say 'fat mincing queen'."

I thought – OK, but didn't he just say 'fat mincing queen'?

No straight person would ever say that, it was hilarious. It was as if he'd just come out to me.

SIR DEREK JACOBI

I came out to my mother when I was at University. I'd fallen in love with somebody and we'd had a row on the way to London, so when I got back home I broke down in front of my mother. When she asked what the matter was, I said, "Mum I'm a homosexual."

She was wonderful. She said, "You're at university, you're in a world you don't understand yet, all young men go through this stage, you can have it both ways, you're growing up."

Anyway, she took it wonderfully, and I remember her saying, "Don't tell dad, don't tell dad." Which presumably *she* did. But it was obvious she knew already.

DAVID HOCKNEY

Well I'm an artist so I had to be honest, I mean I didn't want to deceive anybody really. Sixty years ago I was painting homosexual propaganda.

LORD BROWNE

The very first piece of art I ever bought was a picture by David Hockney. For him to paint those pictures was an act of defiance. I wanted to join in with it.

MATTHEW PARRIS

Heaven knows what my family thought before I told them I was gay. It's not the sort of thing I would want to ask them about really. I suppose they may have guessed, or at least my mother may have guessed, but I had no idea and I never thought there'd be a problem with them. They're a liberal tolerant open family and I always knew there'd be any kind of support I needed and no problems. Anyway, I'm one of those people who doesn't want to talk about sex with their father or mother or brothers or sisters. Family is family, and I wouldn't want my brothers and sisters to talk to me about sex either.

EVAN DAVIS

A key point in my own increasing comfort with being gay was when I went off to the States for a couple years on the East Coast. Everybody there said, "Evan, you must go to the West Coast for the summer!"

When I got to LA it just felt so liberating and I very quickly got a boyfriend because that's what happened in LA. I mean within days, literally days, I had a boyfriend who I was with for the whole summer and beyond. His parents were just so accepting of it and that was quite a revelation to me.

Once I'd been there for a while it was very hard to think of going back to something more oppressed in London, so when I got back from those two years studying in the States I just told my family, and started telling everybody else, and was more public about it.

MATT LUCAS

Well, for me, coming out was something that happened a number of times. I used to fool around with a guy in my teenage years, so I guess he knew, but we never said it. The first person I told was my friend Claire, when I was 19, and she was fine. Then I told my friend Jeremy, "I think I'm bisexual." You know – the old bi now, gay later.

He said, "That's fine, my girlfriend is bisexual," then listed three or four other friends who were also bisexual.

I was furious, absolutely furious. I thought this was my moment of drama but rather like the 'only gay in the village' I was totally undermined by these other stories of gayness.

At least my brother wasn't delighted. When I told *him* I was gay he went, "Oh great!" Like I'd just put the coloured clothes in with the white clothes in the washing machine. You know, "Oh great!"

WILL YOUNG

I went to an all-boys school. It was a boarding school and I played a lot of sport, so it wasn't the place to come out. But when I got to University I fell in love with someone.

I'd always thought I'd fall in love with someone or meet someone and that would lead to me telling my family. So I did. I told a friend in London and my friend told my brother, which was the perfect sort of bomb to throw into the family because my brother was a gossip.

I'd fallen in love with someone who was straight so it was the classic falling in love with someone who wasn't available. But it still did the job for me, which was to bring me out into the world. It was great, but it still took me ten years to get rid of the internalised shame.

QBOY

It was difficult growing up in Basildon. There were no gay clubs, nothing gay there at all. The only way I had of meeting other gay people was by putting a newspaper advert in the lonely-hearts thing in the back of the *Evening Echo*, the local Basildon newspaper, and I met people that way. Often that was very hit or miss because you didn't know who you were meeting. It's a totally blind date situation and I was only like 16 at the time.

Lucy who was also gay, was the driver in our little gay duo and she drove me to this date, but as we approached I wasn't impressed with what he was wearing, it was a very large purple coat. I just thought – oh God, he looks like a Telly Tubby. So I ducked down in the car and was like, "Keep driving, keep driving ."

There were a few of those instances, and then there were

a few where I ended up with men that were much older than me because you never really knew. There aren't many pickings so sometimes you're thrown into the deep end a little when you're really young.

MATTHEW TODD

Once I'd come out, I went on *Gay Pride* marches feeling incredibly proud but there was still this underlying subconscious shame that was making me not feel very good about myself. When I was growing up I was a child who didn't conform to the established gender roles. I was skipping around dancing and singing songs from *The Wizard of Oz* and quickly realised there was something very different about me. I realised I needed to suppress myself to be safe – to try and shut down those mannerisms, shut down those differences.

LORD BROWNE

When I was CEO of BP I was not out. Now that I am I realise that if in a corporate environment you're pretending to be someone different from who you really are, then you're definitely not using all of your brain to do your business. You won't be fully engaged with what the corporation is doing, and you can't be a member of a team unless other people know something about who you are. They don't need to know everything – your bank account or things like that – but they do need to know about your essential personality, such as gender, race, and sexuality. It's part of your fundamental being and people need to know that and participate with it.

MARK McADAM

My immediate family knew I was gay, my close friends knew I was gay, but not the footballers, the sports broadcasters, that side of my life. It was a completely different world, and I ensured as I grew up that there was a very strict line between what I did professionally and what I did personally. About six months before I came out publicly I sat down with one of my closest friends, who at the time was a League One manager, and said to him, "Look, I'm gay."

This was my oldest friend in football, someone I'd known since I was 16. He said, "Look Mark, it really doesn't matter, and I don't think it matters to anybody else. I'm still here, and nothing is going to change."

I walked away from that meeting and thought – that's someone I respect hugely and if he's not got a problem with it why should I care if anyone else has?

LORD PADDICK

My Beautiful Launderette is a very important film in my life. I was watching it on TV and my wife came in just at the scene at the opening of the launderette, where the two boys are making out in the back and his uncle and his acquaintance are at the front door. And rather than my wife's reaction being, "Oh, how disgusting, two men kissing each other," she said, "Oh no, they're going to be caught."

That gave me an indication that if I told her she might actually be sympathetic, and it was within months of that incident, and that film, that I told her I was gay.

Her response was, "Well you obviously need something I can't give you," which I thought was a very grown up approach to things, and she's been a support ever since.

EVAN DAVIS

I didn't go into the BBC screaming, "I'm gay, I'm gay," but once I'd been on screen reasonably frequently the whole issue of newspapers and outing and being exposed came up and in the back of my head I was thinking, do I need to worry about this?

It was 1993 and we were coming out of the 'don't ask, don't tell' period into a time when it was fine to tell people.

I felt I needed to say something so it didn't look like a secret. My colleagues knew, my parents knew, my family and friends knew, but what I didn't want was to read something about myself in the press. So when *Gay Times* asked if I would do an interview I thought, yes, this is my chance, I can be casually out, talking about it before somebody else does.

That was a really good thing to do because once you're out, you're out, and it's easy.

LORD PADDICK

My father nearly had a nervous breakdown and my mother had already indicated her feelings when I broke off a previous engagement. I'd gone home in tears, then rather dramatically put the engagement ring on the glass-top table next to the arm chair I was sitting in. She'd said, "Oh, thank God for that, I thought you were going to tell me you were queer." Which set coming out to my parents back a few years.

Eventually they accepted my sexuality and have welcomed the many and various partners I've had over the years into their home. I don't think either of my parents were particularly happy with it, but then it also took me twenty years before I had enough courage to actually be myself at work.

MARK WARDEL

I never felt the need to come out because in London you didn't really need to and I was never into making political statements about it or anything like that. Then about 20 years ago Boy George came to one of my art openings and said, "I'm going to cover this in my *Sunday Express* column."

My cousins were down from Liverpool. They always knew I was gay and they were excited that this exhibition was going to be mentioned by Boy George, so they went back and told everyone in Liverpool.

On Sunday my aunt and uncle rushed out and bought the *Sunday Express*. George's column started off by saying, "Mark Wardel, better known as Trademark, is well known on the London gay scene for his hot and horny portraits of naked male hunks."

It wasn't even a gay exhibition, though George made it sound like it was, and apparently my auntie was completely shocked. "Does this mean Mark's gay?" she asked.

My cousin said, "Well yes, he is."

My auntie just said, "I hadn't realised."

LORD BROWNE

People say that I'm happier now that I'm out, that I smile more, I laugh more, and maybe that's the case. It's made me feel I have one less big thing to deal with. I can be myself.

LORD CASHMAN

People think you come out once, but actually you never stop coming out. You have to say, "No, that's not my cousin, or my son, that's my husband." "No, I didn't go out with my girlfriend, I went out with my boyfriend." There are always different people and different situations, all to be dealt with.

ZOE LYONS

When it first happened to me onstage, you know, when someone first really had a go at me and yelled, "Lesbian," it was horrible. "Fucking lesbian." "Fucking this." "Fucking that."

The audience weren't with me either, they really weren't. And it just turned into a bloke shouting abuse at me on stage.

I hadn't been going long enough to sort of deal with it and move on, and yeah, that night he won. It was in the *Balham Banana*, which is normally a lovely gig, but not on that particular evening.

It happened to me again recently. Someone shouted out, "Lesbian," and the whole audience turned on the bloke, which was great. It was wonderful. And I now have the experience to deal with it.

But when it first happens it's quite, you know, brutal. It's raw.

CHAPTER NINE

Section 28

MARGARET THATCHER (at the Conservative Party Conference 1987)

"Children who need to be taught to respect traditional moral values are being taught that they have an inalienable right to be gay. All of those children are being cheated of a sound start in life. Yes, cheated!"

MATT LUCAS

The thing about *Section 28* was that it banned the promotion of homosexuality in schools, which was interpreted as meaning *any* mention of homosexuality.

I regard Margret Thatcher and the people who created and endorsed *Section 28* as murderers because they prevented young men from learning how *not* to contract AIDS and die. You have to remember, there was a time when there wasn't a *Section 28*, and then it came in. It wasn't something they inherited, it was something they initiated.

ANGELA EAGLE

There were some very old-fashioned people in the Lords that seemed to be obsessed with what gay men in particular did in bed. They compared it to bestiality and all sorts of things. You wouldn't believe the tone of it.

SHON FAYE

Section 28 ruined people's teenage lives. It was a disgusting piece of legislation. When you were being homophobically bullied, teachers were not allowed to help, they were too afraid to say anything to comfort LGBT pupils. Even in private they were too afraid to tell you that is was OK to be gay.

ANGELA EAGLE

Section 28 caused a massive amount of bullying and unhappiness to an entire generation of people, some of whom would be gay some of whom would just be confused about their sexual orientation, as many people of that age are, and the teachers could do nothing about it.

SHON FAYE

There was a time when my mum phoned the school because somebody had hit me. The teacher told my mum that it was pretty much my own problem and that I should take better care to protect myself around the school. That was one teacher, but I was told by some other teachers to stop acting so flamboyantly.

People should be on guard for homophobic bullying in schools because often you're so ashamed about it you don't want to say. You think telling someone you've been homophobically bullied means telling someone you're gay, and you don't want to do that. So it creates a culture of silence in which the only thing young LGBT people hear about gay sex when they're growing up is as a way to mock you. It's made out to be disgusting and grotesque. You hear about anal sex and blow jobs, because at that age you don't have a clue about how gay men have sex.

The only way I found out about it was through homosexual bullying. I had no one to talk to. One of my closest friends and I received the same taunts, as he was also gay, but we wouldn't even discuss them with each other. We would just pretend it hadn't happened and we didn't feel able to approach any of the teachers.

School environments like that were a product of *Section 28*.

QBOY

My form tutor at the time was quite religious I think, she always had a cross around her neck. I would say to her like, "This is happening, I'm being bullied," and she would actually say, "I'm not able to help you with this."

Just outright denied me the help I needed.

MANJINDER SINGH SIDHU

Along with every young Asian person, my parents, before they'd even had their child, imagined its life, career and marriage. My mother used to always talk about it when I was young. "Oh you're going to be a doctor or a lawyer and then you're going to get a wife and I'm going to be so happy, she'll be able to help me cook."

You're brainwashed with this and it was a lot of burden, a lot of guilt. And with *Section 28* in existence there were no teachers you could talk to about homosexuality.

SHON FAYE

I was never given any kind of advice about HIV or AIDS. I'm struggling to remember how I came to know about it. I'm bisexual and because I had relationships with women first I came to have sex with men a bit later, so I knew through life experience and having gay friends about condom use and stuff like that. But because of *Section 28* no one sat me down and told me that, and it certainly wasn't explained in schools.

QBOY

Back then I was always constantly aware of AIDS and the HIV epidemic. I was always fearful I was going to become positive, and there must have been other kids who felt the same. But we were told nothing about how to protect ourselves.

DAN GILLESPIE SELLS

Being raised by two mums who lived together and my dad, who lived apart, seemed perfectly normal to me. The first time I realised this was something different was when I went to school and I was waiting to meet people's third parent. I'm super proud of them because they did it during the time of *Section 28* when it wasn't so easy to be recognised as a family.

In that particular document, it talks about *not* legitimising this alternative idea of a family. And we were exactly that.

MATTHEW PARRIS

Right from the start in the Conservative party, I said to myself, if I can't be out in the Conservative party (and I couldn't as it would have destroyed my political career), then at least I can use my position for gay issues and for gay equality. You don't have to be gay to do that, and no one can assume that you're gay just because you do it. Lots of straight Conservative MPs joined the *Out* campaign.

LORD SMITH

My politics were always about fighting inequality and injustice and *Section 28* was an absolutely prime example of injustice and inequality that applied specifically to me. I wanted to go into politics because I wanted to change the world. My own favourite anecdote is from when I'd just done my speech in Rugby and had come out. The following week I was in the tearoom in the House of Commons with large numbers of MPs sitting around and Edwina Curry came marching in and saw me. She marched up to me very briskly, as Edwina used to do, and in a very loud voice she said, "Chris, I gather you have come out. Well done."

Then she turned on her heel and marched out. So, there was quite a lot of support from surprising places.

MATTHEW PARRIS

I became a Vice-President of the Conservative Group for Homosexual Equality. It was my way of doing my bit for the cause without doing what I really wanted to do, which was being open about myself.

LORD SMITH

After I came out in 1984, it was about nine or ten years before anyone else in parliament came out, so it felt quite lonely at times. And you must remember the external atmosphere wasn't good.

There was one moment concerning a very reactionary Tory MP for Lancaster, Dame Mary Elaine Kellett-Bowman. The offices of *Capital Gay* newspaper in London had been firebombed the night before. One of the Labour MPs was on his feet in the House of Commons condemning the firebombing of the offices and Dame Kellet-Bowman shouted out, "It was quite right."

So it wasn't a happy atmosphere.

STEPHEN K. AMOS

I remember *Section 28* being touted as this new way of monitoring sex education for young people and not knowing the ramifications of what that actually meant, which was basically banning teachers from discussing homosexuality within the school. I mean that's quite profound.

For any teacher who may have been gay themselves to deal with that legislation is a slap in the face, and to any young child going through the turmoil of finding out who they are and not having access to information, wow that's so damaging. As a piece of legislation by a Conservative government I found it very hard to have a conversation with anyone who was gay, open and Tory.

PAUL GAMBACCINI

Margaret Thatcher was a smart person, she had her Oxford degree and she knew, whatever you think of her, that you had to deal with what's thrown at you. And one of the unexpected things that was thrown at her was AIDS.

Taking advice, she let the people who were experts in that area deal with it. She didn't try to pretend it wasn't happening, she didn't try to pretend – oh it's inconvenient for me. She dealt with the reality. But it was so unfortunate she later chose to throw red meat to the right wing of her party with *Section 28*. I suppose it was the politician in her.

TRIS PENNA

When Margaret Thatcher came to power in 1979 I became a big fan, though of course everyone else hated her. I thought she was fabulous – a woman with a handbag beating up these eurocrats in Brussels. She certainly did the right thing in terms of the early AIDS campaign and I didn't ever view her as a devil or a demon. The only thing she did wrong was *Section 28*, towards the end of her reign – a nasty bit of reactionary behaviour.

LORD SMITH

It was the time of *Section 28* coming in and being argued about furiously on the floor of the House of Commons, but there was one tiny little signal to me that we'd made a lot of progress. It was one of the debates on *Section 28*, and one of the Neanderthal Tories, Nicholas Winterton, was on his feet speaking. I intervened to make a point in opposition to what he was saying and, as I sat down, he looked across at me and he said, "The House has learned to listen to the honourable gentlemen with respect when he talks about these matters."

Just two years earlier he wouldn't have felt the needed to say that. But he felt he had to because we'd made a little bit of progress in establishing a right to speak about these things, even in the House of Commons.

MATTHEW PARRIS

The Labour party was always more ideologically pro-gay, but it was never a gay friendly place, it was quite working class. In lots of ways it was also quite Marxist, and neither working class culture nor Marxist culture has a lot of time for that sort of decadence.

I was taken aside by a very kindly Labour member called Walter Harris – he was deputy chief whip. Basically what he said was, "Just leave it alone, lad. This kind of thing will never get you anywhere in the Conservative party. Just leave it alone."

It was meant in a kindly way.

LORD CASHMAN

In 1988 the Conservative government brought in *Section 28*, which was a hundred years on from when the *Labouchere Amendment* had originally criminalised homosexuality. *Section 28* sent a signal to the LGBT communities to shut up and not be talked about. Certainly not to be talked about in schools and local authorities, and not to be 'promoted', whatever that meant.

PAUL GAMBACCINI

I was asked if I would present one of the episodes of a forthcoming *Channel 4* series called *Out on Tuesday*, which was going to be the first network LGBT television program. I said I wanted mine to be the first program because I thought the program was going to make history, and I was filmed saying that for the first time in my life I lived in a country that had deliberately taken a step backwards in civil rights.

LORD SMITH

The Tories are really interesting because in those days there were a lot of homophobic elements within the party. Let's not forget, it was Tory backbenchers, with encouragement from the then Tory government, that brought in *Section 28*. Some of the things they said in those debates were really hurtful, egged on by the tabloid press.

PAUL GAMBACCINI

Section 28 even affected the AIDS campaign the government

was funding. It said you cannot use government funds to disseminate information promoting homosexual lifestyles, which could easily be interpreted as, "You can't talk about men having sex because that's promoting men having sex."

So even if you're saying, "Don't have sex," you're promoting the idea that some men *do* have sex.

So Ian Mckellen got up during the live Laurence Olivier Awards broadcast and made his heroic speech against *Section 28*....

SIR IAN MCKELLEN (from the stage in 1988)

"I'm here to speak out because I'm one of millions of normal homosexuals who are affected by this new law. *Section 28* is designed, in part, to keep us in our place. Well, it didn't work with me!."

CHRIS SMITH

During the 1987 election there had been a big row about a book called *Jenny Lives with Eric and Martin,* a copy of which had been in a teacher's centre run by and inner-city London education authority. The press had gone bananas about this book and how dreadful it was that this perversion was being taught to children, and all that sort of rubbish. There was a national Conservative party poster at that election – huge billboards, with a photograph of the book on one side of the poster, and on the other side Labour's education policy. Now that's dog whistle politics. That's a really nasty homophobic kind of politics.

MATTHEW PARRIS

I was never much bothered personally by *Section 28*, I was after all a conservative MP. I shared my party's aversion to the loony left, and to some of their strange causes, and to some of the odd groups who they wanted to draw together in a kind of rainbow anti-establishment coalition. I didn't like the idea of indoctrinating children in schools. It hardly happened, but that book did exist, *Jenny Lives with Eric and Martin*.

I don't think I really woke up to quite how offensive *Section 28* was going to seem to a lot of people until I realised it had become a token around which gay people rallied. Once I realised that, I was against it. And I joined all the other people who were against it.

STEPHEN K. AMOS

I would imagine if you're a Tory, apart from campaigning against *Section 28*, if you see it actually become law and you're still within that party you'd have to leave. There is no better way of showing your disgust than by quitting and fighting against it. If the majority of your party has passed this law and you're still sitting on the same table with them then it reminds me of the whole apartheid thing in South Africa.

MATTHEW PARRIS

There were a number of conservative MPs who one just knew were gay. Sometimes one had reason to know because one had seen them somewhere, and sometimes there was just no doubt about it. Some amongst them took a particularity anti-gay stance, perhaps only to defend themselves. I ought to have been able to understand the predicament they were in, but I couldn't. I really disproved of that. I really disapprove of people who persecute their own side and there were some who might have helped so much more than they did.

PAUL GAMBACCINI

A friend reported to me one night with the greatest distress that he'd attended a Tory fund raising dinner in which William Hague, then Leader of the Tory party, interrupted the proceedings to say he had great news, "The Lords have defeated the overturning of *Section 28*."

I mean he actually interrupted a dinner to say what great news it was that *Section 28* had survived.

LORD CASHMAN

I was one of those who helped to lead the campaign against *Section 28*, but we failed and it became law. So a small group of us formed an organisation called Stonewall, which had the aim of ensuring another *Section 28* never happened. To do it we needed finance.

As luck would have it I bumped into Billy Connolly and complained that his manager, John Reed, never returned my calls. Billy said to me, "It's nothing personal, he doesn't return my calls either."

That afternoon John rang me and asked me over for dinner. There was me, Paul Gambaccini, Elton John, John Reed, Ian McKellen, and a couple of others. I talked to Elton about what we wanted to do and he said, "I'll give you £50,000."

He called across the table to John and said, "Michael has been telling me about Stonewall and I'm giving them £50,000."

There was a long pause, and John went, "I'll match it."

PAUL GAMBACCINI

And that was the founding of Stonewall, with the finance achieved in one dinner. And as Ian and Michael walked down John Reed's driveway at the end of that evening I've never seen two happier people in my life. Their dream organisation was off and running.

LORD SMITH

In fact, there was never any prosecution of anyone under *Section 28* – no local authority, no teacher, nobody. However, what did happen was a huge amount of self-censorship, where teachers would feel like they weren't able to give advice and schools felt unable to put a particular book into the school library.

It's the way censorship has worked throughout history – people become afraid to do things, and that was the really insidious thing that *Section 28* brought with it. Getting rid of it from the statute book was one of the very best things that the Labour government did, post 1997.

CHAPTER
TEN

Not thinking straight

DAN GILLESPIE SELLS

There was my biological mum, whose name is Kath, and my other mum, whose name is Dilis. Because my mum was my biological mother we called her mum, and Dilis we called Dilis. I suppose because it's an unusual kind of Irish name, I assumed that everyone else had a Dilis. For me that was the term – dad, mum, Dilis – so I thought, uncle, aunty, grandmother – I thought that was a family role. So actually, when I went to school I realised that not everyone else had one of those.

MATT LUCAS

Homosexuality is about as old as the hills. In fact, the hills were probably making love to each other. But being gay is a new thing, we still have to figure out what gay is. If you're casual about it, then I think people can be casual hearing about it, you know, rather than make a big dramatic thing. There are still places where I will give a goodbye kiss, and places where I won't.

DAN GILLESPIE SELLS

When I was at school, I was bullied for being gay, bullied for being slightly effeminate, bullied for being different, bullied for being into music, bullied for all kinds of different stuff. But I was never bullied because of my parents being two women and that still surprises me.

LORD PADDICK

One of the reasons why I joined the police service was because I thought, well at least my gang is going to be bigger than the other gang if I joined the police. But it was a very homophobic organisation at that time and I again concealed my homosexuality. Having been in the police force for five years I married a woman and we were married for five years, such were the lengths that I went to in order to try and play it straight.

MARK WARDELL

I wouldn't really want to be straight, you know, I think I'm far happier being gay. I mean, like in any situation there are downsides, it's not a complete easy life of bliss or anything like that.

But it's who you are. And as you get older, you get happier, you become more comfortable with who you are. When I was younger, I didn't really know who I was, and I think it's the same with most people. I'm probably happier being gay now than I was when I was in my twenties.

STEPHEN FRY

One of the gifts of being born gay is that you immediately focus on the nature of your sexuality because it's different. One of the curses of being heterosexual is that you don't focus on your sexuality because it's the norm, so you expect your social and sexual relations to be normal and therefore easy. Heterosexual people are very annoyed that it's very hard if you're heterosexual, for a girl to find a boy or for a boy to find a girl, for them to know each other, be at ease with each other, understand and respect each other, discover how each other's bodies work and what their needs, rhythms and desires are. It's a nightmare.

All my straight friends told me through my teenage years, "Oh God, you're so lucky, you go to bed with people of the same sex, it's easy – you know what they like, you both know what it's about."

Being straight is like visiting another planet.

TOM ROBINSON

I think the main difference between my own situation,

ending up married to a woman and with kids, compared to the pre-legalisation days when many gay men were forced to get married and have kids as a way of fitting into society, is that my wife knew me as an out gay man at the time and that's why she liked me. She didn't have a relationship with me *despite* me being gay. A big part of the attraction was the fact that I *was* gay.

I frequently get asked, "When did you stop being gay?"

The answer is — I never did. I never stopped liking men. I've always liked men for as long as I can remember going back to early childhood and I'm sure I always will. I have a preference for men, I've always had a preference for men. I just happened to fall in love with someone of the wrong sex, that's all.

STEPHEN FRY

It's worth looking at the power of words in this issue of gay acceptance, liberation and normalisation. Throughout the world in history, whether it was Greece or the Far East or South America (for example in Polynesia where there has always been an acceptance of gay behaviour or same sex relationships), there was never a word to describe someone of being somehow genetically in that identity. In our culture too, the word didn't really exist until André Gide, who is considered to be the first person to use the word as a noun. He referred to a person as 'homosexual', as in saying "I am a homosexual, making it belong to the person rather than to the person's behaviour.

STEVE BLAME

When I started at MTV, before I was on air, they told me, "We just want to have a discussion about whether you're allowed to be gay."

I asked, "How am I supposed to deal with this point?"

The Austrian press secretary of MTV piped up and said, "Everyone on television in Europe is gay."

One of the Americans said, "Oh really?"

"Yes! Everyone!" she told them, then winked at me as I left the room as if to say, "I just made that up."

I survived. But later on, when I had a chat show on MTV, they decided it was a bit too gay so the heads of MTV America came over and met up with the heads of MTV Europe. In Amsterdam they went to a restaurant and while they were talking about MTV the waiter overheard and said, "Oh! Steve Blame, my favorite presenter."

When they came back to London they told me, "Seems like you're really popular."

What they didn't know was that I'd had sex with that waiter two weeks before when I was in Amsterdam.

ANGELA EAGLE

It was strange. When I came out to John Prescott, who's straight, he was like, "Yeah! I've known that for years." But that wasn't the case with Chris Smith.

Because he was the first parliamentarian to have come out, I wanted to ask him some advice about how to do it. But again, because he was secretary of state it took me ages to get an appointment before we ended up having an evening meal at a restaurant.

We got all the way to the dessert before I managed to say, "Oh, by the way, I'm gay."

He was gob-smacked. And when I went to see Peter Mandelson he was gob-smacked too.

All the heterosexual men were like, "Yeah, we know," And the gay men hadn't really noticed.

LORD BROWNE

When I was presenting my book, *The Glass Closet*, at the Hay

Festival, a young man in the audience got up and said, "Well, John, I want to say this to you, I'm in your business, but I was with a competitor company, and we all knew you were gay in the early 2000s. The only problem nobody was brave enough to go up and tell you that you were gay."

I thought that said it all really. It was about the way in which business works, and the way in which people preserve respectful privacy, probably for the wrong reasons. This is a very English conversation, which occurs on two levels. The first level is that nothing, apparently, is known, and the second level is that everything is known. And a very English conversation took place.

STEPHEN FRY

People will always accuse those they disagree with of preaching. And for those who have been the public face of gay liberation, whether to fight for it aggressively or quietly has caused a great deal of argument as to which is the right approach.

PETER TATCHELL

Stonewall was essentially the suffragists, the ones who lobbied governments and did things through the respectable traditional routes. Outrage was more the suffragettes, we took direct action, we confronted homophobes and institutions face-to-face. For eight years in the Nineties, the Archbishop of Canterbury, Dr George Cary, refused to meet or have a dialogue with any LGBT organisations. He wouldn't even talk to the Lesbian and Gay Christian Movement – many of whose members belonged to his own Anglican church. *Outrage* tried to have a dialogue and we were rebuffed. So after having the door slammed in our face for so many years we went to Canterbury Cathedral on Easter Sunday to challenge the archbishop face-to-face. We didn't interrupt any of the sacred part of the service like hymns and prayers, we waited until Dr Cary began his sermon – then seven of us walked into the pulpit holding up placards criticising Dr Cary's support for legal discrimination against LGBT people. I did a sort of brief alternative sermon simply criticising the fact that the Archbishop was justifying discrimination against our community.

MATTHEW TODD

With a magazine like *Attitude* you want people to buy it so you need to entertain them. I was very aware that celebrities sell magazines. Sexy men on the cover also sell magazines, but under my editorship I tried to steer away from that a little bit. Someone challenged me over it, they said, "You wouldn't put Stephen Fry on the cover would you?"

So we did. And not many people bought it.

I and don't think it was a reflection of whether people like Stephen Fry or not, it was a reflection of what gay men wanted from a gay magazine. By the time *Attitude* came along there was a desire for entertainment and a move slightly away from politicising everything. But actually that's more my interest so I tried to make *Attitude* a bit more political. I would put a sexy pop star with his shirt off on the cover with intelligent articles inside, interviews with David Cameron or Tony Blair, that type of thing.

MATT LUCAS

Homosexual is a brilliant word because there is something disdainful about it. It's sort of 'handle with tweezers', isn't it? Also, the thing I like about 'homosexual' is that it's quite a sibilant word, so even straight people sound a bit gay when they say it. On the other hand, I think 'queer' is quite a helpful word, because we're a bit queer in the old-fashioned sense of the word, "It's a queer thing we do, given what everyone else does."

So I quite like the word queer, though I would never actually use it to describe myself.

MANJINDER SINGH SIDHU

I decided to write a book called *Bollywood Gay* because there was nothing available here for people like myself. It was for people like myself who wanted that Bollywood lifestyle, or marriage, or family, that our parents envisioned. But it's about doing it in a gay way, a self-help book about how to get rid of the shame and guilt and have inner confidence. I added a part with 13 different languages because when I came out to my parents there was nothing in their literature in Punjabi or Hindi, and even the NHS doesn't have anything like that. And because I get Arabic speakers contacting me, I added an Arabic section which deals with what to say when they want to come out, and what to do. They can present it to their parents, or just read it out to them.

STEPHEN FRY

If I were growing up now my awareness would be very different because I would know straight away that I was gay because the internet lays it all out with apps and all kinds of things to assure me that not only am I gay but that I fit precisely into this category of gay man who likes this kind of thing. Whether I was a 'bear' or an 'otter' or a 'twink' – all these extraordinary words that are used to categorise us.

DAVID HOCKNEY

When I was young I picked Diaghilev as a mentor because I'd read biographies of him. He was picking up cadets in St Petersburg; he was a Russian aristocrat and Russian aristocrats could do what they wanted. He was always open about his gayness. I mean he didn't try to hide it at all, and

I knew it, even in England. He was a living bohemian and because I lived in Bohemia I knew people there and they didn't care about whether you were gay or not. There was a Bohemia in New York and there was one in LA, and there were a lot of gay people in Bohemia. They've killed Bohemia now because of money, and I think that's sad. Now you need money to lubricate life, but Bohemia wasn't about money. It was about lots of new ideas and things. Bohemians always had that.

THE REVEREND ANDREW FORESHEW-CAIN

I can't name tunes, but in the early Nineties, before I'd met Steven, I used to go clubbing rather a lot, so quite a lot of house. I danced with my t-shirt off in clubs all over the West End. I was a curate in South London and we used to go to the *Fridge* and *Heaven*, those kinds of places, and dance till five in the morning. Then back home as quickly as I could, threw my cassock over my sweaty top, and time for first communion.

DAVID HOCKNEY

The first real gay bar I found was in LA in 1964. There were big gay bars in 1964 in California. Oh, it was amazing, California in the Sixties. That's why I went to LA, because of the gay thing. And the colour. You got more colour in California. And I met Christopher Isherwood there too. I had always admired him

DAN GILLESPIE SELLS

I so much admire Ian McKellen. I think he's great. He's fun to be around, but also he's an amazing advocate for LGBT issues. It's nice to have an older role model like that, though I've become good friends with a lot of them now and it seems a bit weird to call them role models. But it's brilliant that they're out there, and it's brilliant there are lots of young new role models too, like Olly Alexander, and a bunch of cool new kids coming out the modern way – not a big deal, not a tabloid story – they're there, they're proud, and they're great. No shame attached to it.

OLLY ALEXANDER

I've had a lot of therapy so I think I'm pretty good at talking about shame – toxic shame – it affects so many things in your life. But I think because I've had a lot of therapy and I've tried to unpack the reasons behind why I feel shame about certain things, it's set me on a course that's kind of, well – where there's a better future ahead. So yes – I think you can overcome shame for sure.

JASON PRINCE

One of the turning points for me in not being ashamed of my sexuality came from talking to Richard, the lead singer of *Right Said Fred*. Each time they came to the studio he chatted with me. They recorded this really outrageous song called 'I'm Too Sexy', which was about male models. I thought the song was absolutely fantastic, but in my naivety, because they were three big muscle guys, it never struck me that they might be gay. Then one day I was talking to Richard when he said, "Sorry girl, I got to go."

I felt myself go red because nobody had ever spoken to me like that before. It was the first time I really noticed that somebody who didn't look gay, didn't look like Boy George or Marilyn, could be a real man and still be gay.

BARONESS BARKER

In 1985 I did that thing you should never do, I picked a book by its cover. I'd walked into the *Feminist Library* by the Embankment tube and seen a book by an author I'd never heard of. I took it home, sat down, and read the opening line:

"Like most people I lived for a long time with my mother and father. My father liked to watch the wrestling, my mother liked to wrestle, it didn't matter what..." And off we went.

For the first time there it was in writing, about lesbians as opposed to gay men, and we could be funny and interesting at the same time as putting up with an awful lot of terrible treatment.

Later I was in *Gay Is the Word*, the gay bookstore in Marchmont Street in Bloomsbury, and when I mentioned the book to the guy on the desk, he said, "The lady who wrote is at the back."

I went up and said, "This is brilliant. I just think it's wonderful." And for the one and only time in my life I behaved like a pop fan.

MATTHEW TODD

I was a huge Madonna fan. You know, when you're 16 years old and you've read in the papers day-in day-out that being gay is disgusting and immoral and that basically gays should be shot, which some politicians seemed to be saying almost literally. To see Madonna come up onto the stage and tell everyone to fuck themselves if they didn't like it. That was just so empowering

Actually, she wasn't really that explicit about it but part of what she had to say was that it was OK to be gay. That doesn't seem like a big deal now but at that time it was radical, and I became completely obsessed with her and her gay dancers. I became a massive fan. I got to interview her in the end which was a really nice full-circle moment for me.

BARONESS BARKER

LGBT people have always been very adaptable. We've always met the world as it is, and we've survived. These days some of the older generation are maybe a bit walking-wounded, but I think the best of us want to change the world so that the generation of kids who are coming up don't carry all that baggage, don't have to negotiate, don't have to choose between themselves and their family, or their religion, but can just be accepted and valued as individuals within their community. That's what we have to work towards.

MATTHEW TODD

There's a perception that everything is fine now, that young people who've grown up in a more caring, more tolerant era, are having an amazing time. I'm sure it's better than it was, and there are huge numbers of people having an amazing time and feeling relaxed about their sexuality, but there are still a lot of people who are struggling, a lot of young people too.

I put out an online request to speak to people outside of London and I had so many people respond. Loads of people saying they were having a great time but there were some really shocking stories, like the young man who wrote to tell me that every day he would be homophobically abused. He was known as the local queer and would be spat at; he would get abuse on the bus every day.

Another gay man wrote to tell me that his stepfather wouldn't let him have dinner with his siblings in case he turned them gay; and would sometimes block his car in the drive just to make life difficult for him.

When we realise we're gay, if we've absorbed that negative message from society saying we're not good enough, we tend to accept it – accept it as our lot, as if we deserve it.

SHON FAYE

Although things are better in terms of legal rights, they gotten worse in some material ways for younger gay people. I can understand that for older gay men who have seen decriminalisation, who have seen empowering of legal rights, and gay people in politics, it looks very positive, and in once sense it is. But legal rights aren't everything.

What's happened is that people are sold this myth that things are progressing. Governments and companies that market to gay people like to sell that idea, but in fact a quarter of homeless youths in the UK are LGBT.

MATTHEW TODD

We went through a huge commercialisation of gay culture in the Nineties. For a long time people thought that was really positive because the concept of the pink pound meant gay bars springing up everywhere. Old Compton Street was seen as this desirable place and major companies were advertising in gay magazines and would do gay campaigns with rainbow colours. But when you see some of the bigger companies that have floats at *Gay Pride* you can't help but feel it's very hollow. Do they really have an engagement with it or are they just there to flog a few units?

JASON PRINCE

I perform at most of the *Gay Pride* events and nearly every town now has one. Last year I performed on the main stage at seven or eight of them and through the summer I felt like I was living and performing *Gay Pride* nonstop. The smaller ones are absolutely marvelous because they're still full of community spirit. But the larger ones have become big business, like everything else does eventually – who can sell the most tickets?

When I first started singing at Brighton *Pride* a few years ago it was a completely non-commercial event. But now it's one of the biggest, with famous people on the main stage. There's the whole of Preston Park and they sell tickets. It's ridiculously packed, not just with gay people but with everybody.

ANGELA EAGLE

I'm worried that *Pride* is becoming too commercialised and being taken over by corporate lobbyists. People are marching under corporate banners rather than community banners. The gay community is being fractured and fragmented in a new way.

One of the things we mustn't forget when we're thinking of LGBT history is how important vibrant community organisations are. They're really the key to the whole thing – somewhere that gay people can meet and know they'll be supported. With the huge inflation in property prices, many iconic gay venues are being forced to close, and granting alternative uses to pubs that have been there for years, that's a real problem.

JASON PRINCE

Last year at Brighton, instead of the main stage, I was asked to sing at the street party, which isn't ticketed. It's a separate event from the big show in Preston Park and a lot of people prefer it. Like starting *Pride* all over again but with street parties, and keeping it more gay.

MATTHEW TODD

It's interesting what's happened with Jeremy Joseph and his successor at G.A.Y. They would get these huge superstars, you know, like Lady Gaga, Mariah Carey, Madonna and all these different types of people, which would attract straight kids to come to see them too. And there was often controversy about whether they should be allowed in because, obviously, they want to keep the crowd gay.

CHAPTER
ELEVEN

God and other gay chat

STEPHEN FRY

Homophobia is a peculiar thing. I have never really understood why anybody would be so obsessed with other peoples' sexuality when that sexuality is consensual and causes nothing but happiness among those who practice it. A lot of homophobic people want to make other people homophobic but gay people don't want to make other people gay. The idea that they do has been very destructive to the acceptance of homosexuality.

MANJINDER SINGH SIDHU

In Indian religion it doesn't say homosexuality is a sin. It doesn't really mention it much. I mean in Hinduism you had hermaphrodites, transgender, lesbians, gays, all these things existed – but it was only when the British colonisers came and brought *Section 377* and outlawed it did that change. But in our religion it doesn't say anything against it. It says, be a good human being, procreate if you can, and pass on good genes and good values. It says marriage is between two souls and it doesn't say it's a man and a woman. So there's no shame about it as you have in the Abrahamic religion.

LORD CASHMAN

Sometimes I think we have to work with religions for them to understand that it is not right in any religion to encourage persecution or discrimination, or to diminish another life – and I say this as a born-again atheist. If you really do believe in God and the afterlife, then how dare you commit the blasphemy of taking the place of God.

STEPHEN FRY

I don't want to overstate the role of the church here because, in a sense, it's more recently that the various churches or religions have become the public enemies of the acceptance of homosexuality. It was a purely cultural and social thing before because the church didn't really have much to say about it. Things have changed because the church understood that the norm was pushed by the state.

LORD CASHMAN

There are elements within all religions that are progressive, and we need to work with them, and encourage them, but equally recognise the complex situations of lesbian, gay, bi, or trans people to whom religion is central to their lives. Sometimes those people face persecution, not only within their religious community but within the LGBT community as well.

THE REVEREND ANDREW FORESHEW-CAIN

The conservative evangelicals in the church of England say the bible says that being gay is wrong – homosexual genital acts, as they like to refer to them, are condemned in scripture and it's not possible to be a practicing homosexual and a Christian. They take a very strict biblical line based on seven verses in the whole of Christian scripture and they promote it quite vigorously.

STEPHEN FRY

It's astonishing that another human should dare to tell me what to do with any part of my body whether it's my penis or my middle finger or my nose or my ears. We're going to be on this earth for a very short time and it seems to me we should be trying the fruit of every tree of every garden and orchard and forest because they're put their for our pleasure and interest. Some of them will be poisoned, some of them will be highly addictive and dangerous, some of them will be so delicious that we'll not be able to work or do anything else, and some of them will just be dull. But surely it would be a sad thing to come to the end of one's life, lying on one's death bed saying, "Oh, I never tried that."

QBOY

Young guys are trying everything, watching things on the internet that they would never even dream of before you know. You've got probably 14 year old boys self-fisting themselves at home because they've been watching it on *X Tube* or some porn website, and that's something that would never have entered their minds had they not had the internet. It feels like everything is happening to people much faster and much younger, but they don't have the emotional maturity or experience that comes along with what they're doing. I think – well if you're doing that now at 15 what the hell are you going to be doing at 40?

DAVID HOCKNEY

Well I'm 79. And I'm quite healthy actually. I mean, I stand up to paint six or seven hours a day. A while back I was in Holland Park and sat down and was watching some black rabbits in the park, and some blackbirds and magpies came down. I was smoking a cigarette and three girls go running by saying, "Oh no, no, no, no, no, no."

I sat there and thought, they think they're very healthy but they haven't noticed the rabbits or the magpies. They're obsessed with their own bodies but I thought I was healthier. To be gay you have to be tolerant but loads of gay people don't smoke now and they've become rather intolerant of smokers and drinkers and all kinds of people.

ANGELA EAGLE

I'm a big fan of David Hockney. We're both from Yorkshire and he has his studio in Bridlington, where I was born. But he's a militant pro smoker about which I'm sure we'd quarrel.

Though it doesn't seem to have affected his longevity because it's fantastic work that he's doing.

STEPHEN FRY

As a teenager, I only had books. I lived in the country and my parents had a house that was miles from the nearest shop and there was this tiny little television that was hidden away except for great occasions like the death of Churchill. So what one was thrown upon was looking at books in the library, some of them rather depressing, others rather good. I got good at decoding the library's file of 'subject matter'. Like that you could find titles that showed gay promise – for example, a biography about a literary set in Tangier. But my real obsession was Oscar Wilde, and the gay Greek poet Cavafy was a also big influence on me, as were Allen Ginsberg and Walt Whitman. In the mainstream there was Gore Vidal who wrote *The City and The Pillar*, an extraordinarily frank book about homosexuality. And John Rechy who wrote *City of Night*.

I don't think there was a British equivalent to *City of Night* which was high class gay pulp fiction. In Britain, gay writers were a more literary lot, like TC Worsley, who wrote *Flannelled Fool*, a wonderful gay confession. He was literary editor of *The New Statesman* which was much more upper middle class.

In Britain there were no working class gay novelists.

ANGELA EAGLE

Working class people have always been characterised as somehow lumpen and never having advanced views about anything.

My mum and dad were from Sheffield, my mum was a seamstress and my dad was in the print trade and were just very liberal in their attitudes to all of these issues. They learned constantly and didn't keep rigid views, so as they grew up and got more politically sophisticated they just changed with the times and had enlightened attitudes. I think that a lot of working class people think that way, it's just a caricature to say that they don't.

It was resolutions from the *National Union of Mineworkers* that lead the statute book being wiped clean of discriminatory legislation against LGBT people. Who would have predicted that?

The miners were being abused and attacked by the police they saw the same thing happening to the gay world in London. They realised that solidarity would help, so they moved resolutions that led directly to the changes.

STEPHEN FRY

Generally speaking Americans were ahead of us on matters of sex, and a bombshell exploded with the *Kinsey Report*, which flattened the Eisenhower world of milk and cookies and buzz cuts. The Kinsey report disclosed an extraordinary prevalence of homosexual behavior among all kinds of American men, most of them apparently straight.

The nation had to face that we're all human and that a big part of being human is the sexual impulse. And when the sexual impulse is directed towards your own gender in a society that doesn't accommodate it, there's going to be a huge amount of friction. And there was.

It coincided with the friction that came out of rock and roll and Vietnam and an explosion of other alternative lifestyles.

TOM ROBINSON

The big difference from when I was a teenager is that you can find information, there is counseling, there is help, there are helplines, the help is there. If you break your leg you go to the A and E department and you get it set. If you fall ill physically in any number of ways you can seek treatment.

But if you're broken inside, if you're suffering from crippling depression, the whole British stiff upper lip thing tells you to just man up, to get over it, and that's when people jump in front of trains and off bridges and take overdoses. The other thing looking back on all those years is how casually I tried to take my own life in my teens, because today the single biggest killer of men between 20 and 45 isn't road accidents, isn't disease, isn't alcohol, isn't violent crime – it's suicide.

LORD PADDICK

I've been speaking in the House of Lord lately about Prep, the drug that can prevent HIV. The government isn't prepared to fund it and that's a very important issue. I feel passionate about it which is why I speak up. But one of health minister's arguments against funding Prep was, "What will the *Daily Mail* say?

MATTHEW TODD

The *Daily Mail* and the *The Sun* – unless my parents for bringing them into the house!

That whole gay interaction with consumerism and capitalism and the market is really complicated. In lots of ways it's been really positive because people have seen there's a certain amount of money in the LGBT community and that perhaps unfortunately has driven a certain amount of the liberation we've seen, just as knowing there are votes in gay people, you might argue, is why David Cameron was so much behind equal marriage. But on the other hand I think it can be difficult for gay actors because capitalism is the main reason why it's so unusual to see mainstream leading gay characters in films, and why leading actors don't come out more often. But we're also we are our own worst enemy. For instance, with the film *Pride*. I was really disappointed that such an amazing and really important film wasn't better supported by the LGBT community. I don't think it did as well as it could have done and that sends a signal to the film industry that stories about gay people don't make money – so why should they make them?

MATT LUCAS

You used to get these late-night gay movies on Channel 4. The two I remember were the Derek Jarman movies, which were very admirable, and what he was doing was very brave, but very arty, and oh so bleak. I couldn't really connect with them. I remember asking David Walliams if he had ever seen *Sebastiane,* and he went, "Yes actually, that's my favourite Latin movie."

The other film was *Maurice*, the EM Forster movie, with James Wilby and Hugh Grant. I had a video tape of it which I would hide away. I'm sure I labelled it with something else, like *That's Life*, or something I knew nobody else would want to put in the VCR. I would watch that film repeatedly.

BARONESS BARKER

In 1990, bless them, the *BBC* filmed my favourite book, *Oranges are Not the Only Fruit*. It was wonderful, with Charlotte Colman and a cast of Lancashire character actors, with Kenneth Cranham playing the messianic preacher. It presented us in a quirky, funny, endearing way. Not somewhere stuck out on our own, looking a bit weird, but as part of an overall community. And I remember going to work the following morning and sitting down at lunchtime and there were people, who were not gay, who had watched this television program and really enjoyed it.

Flip forward then to 1998 and I was standing in a friend's apartment. She was an 85-year-old New York, Jewish lesbian. I looked at her bookshelves (I can't help myself from looking at bookshelves), and I just said, "Oh, Oranges."

She replied, "I love that book."

She had no more idea what life was like in Lancashire than flying there, but I asked why she liked it, and she said, "I wish that book had been around for me to read when I was a little girl."

STEPHEN FRY

Yes, so many wonderful books. There was always something in the library with which a curious, worried, upset and excited adolescent could affirm and vindicate his aberrant sexuality.

MARK WARDEL

Now that it's politically correct to be pro-gay, even people who don't like the idea say it's fabulous. Back in the Seventies it was so different; there was a lot of hostility towards being gay. Which made, for instance, what Bowie did by coming out all the more remarkable, though looking at it now there seems to have been an air of calculated publicity about it. But there was obviously truth in it because it's documented he had relationships with men. So he absolutely was, if not gay, bisexual, and possibly leaning more towards the gay side. Maybe he became more interested in the heterosexual side as time went on, but I think it was a bit of a trial, because he very much came out as gay and then bisexual, which was certainly an enormous help to our generation in difficult times. So it's a shame he went back on it because it betrayed a lot of those people.

PETER TATCHELL

Soon after I came out in 1969 I resolved to do my bit to help the struggle for LGBT human rights and freedom. I never set out to make it a lifelong commitment, it's just something that evolved over time. I got quite good at it and worked with many wonderful people who helped bring us to the place where we are today, where Britain is a fundamentally different country from 50 years ago. But my half century of activism has come at a personal price. I've had pretty much non-stop death threats, hate mail, and actual physical assaults on my home and on my person. And it's been really difficult to sustain a personal relationship in that kind of atmosphere and with the level of commitment I have.

STEPHEN FRY

Well we can't all fulfill who we're supposed to be in terms of the various ambitions we might have, but we should always aim at the simple ambition of being the best of what we are – the best Stephen Fry possible – the best 'you' that you can possibly be.

That you could be stopped from being that by another person's prejudice is outrageous. After all, a racist can't make a black man's skin white, but in the past homophobes have tried to make gay people straight. And that's a monstrous thing.

CHAPTER
TWELVE

Advances

MATTHEW TODD

On election night in 1997 I went to G.A.Y. where they played the results live on the big screen. It was packed. And every time a Tory lost a seat everyone would cheer apart from a couple of lone Tory guys. As Labour votes mounted up everyone was ecstatic. We felt like it was a fight for our lives, and at that time it probably was. I don't think things would have happened as quickly if Labour hadn't gotten in.

LORD SMITH

Tony Blair, when we began that whole series of really rather wonderful reforms including lowering the age of consent to 16, was really nervous about doing any of it. He was worried about what the public impact would be, what the press would think. He took a test case to the European Court so he could stand up and say, "Our hand is being forced, we have to do this."

Once it was done, of course, there wasn't a huge public outcry. People rather liked the idea.

ANGELA EAGLE

When I first came into government I felt that public acceptance and attitudes were well ahead of where the government and the legislation were at that time. Attitudes outside of Parliament had changed a lot. Parliament was lagging because we'd had a government that either didn't want to address it or wanted to use it for their own political advantage.

MATTHEW TODD

I think it would have been helpful if Peter Mandleson had spoken about his sexuality in the Nineties. Being a politician high up in the Labour party at that time must have been utterly horrendous, especially with the right wing media saying Labour was the party of gays that want to kind of destroy families and kill your children. But it would have been great to see Mandelson come out earlier and be there as a figurehead. He would have received so much love for that.

ANGELA EAGLE

I think that the LGBT community should demand more than tolerance. Because the implication of that word is that we will tolerate you. I think we're probably beyond that now in the UK and certainly in younger generations it isn't an issue at all, and that's fantastic and long may it continue.

MARK McADAM

Recently, I got asked to attend and play in a gay football tournament. Afterwards, I didn't know which were the gay teams and which were the heterosexual ones. And that was great, because it wasn't about sexuality, it was about people who were comfortable with themselves and their surroundings. They were there to do just one thing and that was to play football. It was fascinating that the gay element of the tournament was the least important thing, yet it was the thing that had brought everyone together.

EVAN DAVIS

I think my career has been mildly helped by being gay. In the media, being interesting is an asset, particularly if it's not a distracting sort of interesting. And being gay, it's sad to say, was one of the more interesting things about me. It was basically a feature, not a problem.

As a feature it was mildly helpful. In the world of the BBC, or the world of the media, I don't think you encounter much direct homophobia. To be honest it's been a fairly comfortable journey. I've felt very much in friendly surroundings. I've never really felt any overt or even covert hostility. And that's quite a thing to say isn't it, I mean for a county where it was illegal 50 years ago.

MARK McADAM

With Sam Stanley, Rugby has beaten football to have the first Premier League player come out. It also has Gareth Thomas, the former captain of Wales, and Nigel Owens, one of the world's top referees. Within sport in general there's been amazing progress over people being able to come out. Adidas have something in their contracts to say, if one of their sponsored athletes comes out, it won't affect them, they'll still get sponsored, still get supported in exactly the same way. I think that's so important.

EVAN DAVIS

In the Eighties and early Nineties there were the lesbians and the gays. But, you were in your group, and you would go to those bars. And everyone in the bars would be gay so you were on safe terrain in terms of trying to get people's attention and everybody knew where they stood.

You would have nights with your heterosexual friends but they would probably not be the same as your homosexual friends and you would compartmentalise everything. That had a kind of simplicity and security about it. But now, it's completely different. I notice from young people, they seem to mix everything up more, which has its advantages. It makes for a much more pleasant social environment because you have a more varied and diverse crowd. The last 50 years of changing the social and legal framework has allowed people to be themselves rather than pretending they're something else. And I do think we're all better when we're ourselves.

MARK McADAM

At the Olympic Games in Rio in 2016, there were a series of

great iconic sporting moments. One of the most personal ones for me was Lee Pearson, at the opening ceremony of the Paralympic Games, leading out Team GB.

To see, not only a gay man leading Team GB out, but someone who had been selected by the team to lead them. It was huge.

The other moment which really stood out was the road race walker Tom Bosworth, who finished sixth, proposing to his partner of nearly five years on *Copacabana Beach*. That was such an iconic image, to see him down on one knee in the sand, having competed at the highest level, and then about to take on the next journey in life and get married.

Q BOY

My father is from the Canary Islands and is a very traditional macho man. So he's never been totally been comfortable with my sexuality. He loves me and he shows me he loves me and he's wonderful in many other ways, but it's not exactly his most conformable subject.

He'd never seen me perform, even at the height of what I was doing when I was touring all over the world, but then I suddenly got booked to perform at Maspolomas *Pride* in Gran Canaria, and he came across from his island together with his girlfriend and my sister.

I came off stage after performing on the main stage with a full set of dancers and it was a really good performance, and he was like, "Marcos that was brilliant, you are really brilliant."

He'd never said anything like that to me in my life so I was over the moon with his reaction. I was really happy that he recognised my talent and my work even though it was at *Gay Pride*. He'd probably never even been to a gay club, so for him to come to the event and then to watch me and have that reaction made me really happy.

MATT LUCAS

I think the normalisation of being gay began when Michael Cashman went into *EastEnders*. We look back on those two gay characters now and it was quite thinly written, but it was a radical progressive brave thing for the BBC to do at the time, they had so much abuse for doing it, other shows wouldn't have survived.

Before that, the image of homosexuality when I was still a child, in the Seventies and Eighties, was that gay people were all incredibly exotic and flamboyant, like Quentin Crisp, or John Inman's Mr. Humphrey, with that camp voice.

STEPHEN FRY

I went to interview a man who trains gay people to lose their gay voice. It's a fascinating fact of linguistics that across cultures and linguistic groups – French, English, German, Slavic, Arabic, Chinese, right across the world – there is a distinctive camp voice – not everyone has it of course, but we all know that a great many people do. And that makes one ask the question – is there some kind of genetic thing that gives you those splashy S's, that camp way of speaking. So I went to find out from this chap in Hollywood who trains young men to lose their gay voice.

He does it principally with actors so they can have a wider range of parts to play. There was one quite well-known actor who used to appear in all those vampire-type TV shows. As he's not come out, I shan't name him, but he did have quite a camp voice. And now he doesn't.

Whether he uses it just for acting and reverts to his camp voice at home, I have no idea. But I do in know that now, in films, he has a nice new butch voice. Well, not exactly butch, but at least it doesn't have those splashy S's anymore.

I really don't know where they from, those splashy 'S's. It's not from men trying to sound like women because women don't have them. It's considered effeminate. But it certainly isn't feminine.

JULIAN CLARY

When I was 17 I was told by everyone that of all the things that were going to be a problem in my life, it would be my voice and my mannerisms. It's true they might have got in the way of other carers but somehow in comedy they worked.

STEPHEN FRY

Gay people like all members of minorities can be self-oppressing and they can be judgmental about other members of their own community. So you get gay people who get angry with people for being incredibly camp. I got very cross with *The Independent* once when they did one of their lists about who are the most influential gay people and they picked on someone who was in a reality TV program as being a negative example because he was very camp – and I thought that was outrageous. You're not a 'better' gay just because you're straight-acting.

JULIAN CLARY

My voice and mannerisms could be used to my advantage, as did talking graphically about gay sex. I found I could only really talk about myself, so whatever I'd been up to I would put that in and talk about it on stage, and because there was a lot of friction around, especially with the police, that was always good comedy value – you know, right wing police and entrapment and homophobia – those were always good areas to be funny about.

LORD CASHMAN

There's been an incredible shift in policing attitudes. It was a lot to do with changes in the law but it's also about the way the law used to be enforced, like the entrapment of gays by pretty policemen. What's incredible now is that you see LGBT people marching in their uniforms, policewomen and policemen. These are the people who have changed attitudes in places where beforehand it would have been considered incredible and unachievable. It's been done by personal determination – that's why policing attitudes have changed – colleagues have turned around to one another and said, "Oh come on."

PETER TATCHELL

Another watershed moment was the formation of Outrage, the direct action LGBT rights group in 1990. It came into existence because we'd had enough. We were fed up with the way in which the police were persecuting us, not protecting us. So we decided to form Outrage.

There were about 30 of us, and we decided we'd use the tactics of the suffragettes. We would use non-violent direct action to challenge the government and other powers in society who were responsible for our ongoing persecution and oppression.

MATTHEW TODD

Because of my classic self-loathing, when I was young I didn't like Peter Tatchell. I was reading the newspapers which portrayed him as public enemy number one and I agreed with gays who said, "Stop rocking the boat, you should be grateful." It's a phase that a lot of us have gone through and I've since told him and apologized. I'm happy now to be a big supporter.

TOM ROBINSON

I think what Peter Tatchell has done has been both very brave and very wise. He's founded a human rights foundation and he stands for human rights of all kinds across the board. Not just for queer rights. He's confronted dictators and got beaten up by secret police and all the rest of it, but not purely on the issue of gay sexuality, even though that his main thing. It's the Peter Tatchell Human Rights Foundation. And like the *Tom Robinson Band*, it aims have been to make society more just in every way, not just for LGBT people. In the band, it had to be like that because I was the only gay member. Human rights were something we could all agree on.

PETER TATCHELL

In 2003 a gay man brought a case in the European Court of Human Rights claiming that the provisions of the 1967 *Sexual Offences Act* were discriminatory. And it was as a result of his particular case that the Labour government then decided not only to address the discrimination that he had suffered but also to remove all other discrimination in the criminal law.

LORD CASHMAN

I said in the House of Lords, in the debate around the 2003 *Sexual Offences Act*, that as a young 18-year-old going to these clubs or these pubs in Earls Court, the law didn't protect me. The law didn't allow me to come out on the street and smile at another man and talk to him. The law penalised me. And the law was used that way right up until the late Nineties. But when it was signalled by politicians that the laws had to change and that it was no longer acceptable, the police moved swiftly to fall in line with it.

ELTON JOHN

I believe that you go in and talk to people from both political parties, and deal with religious organisations who don't believe that what you're doing is right, and you talk to them, and you solve the problem by saying, "Listen. Here I am. I'm not a person from outer space. I'm a normal human being that wants love and respect just like anybody else."

LORD SMITH

One of the government departments which has been most ready to accept diversity within the work place has been the ministry of defence and the armed services, which is a massive change. If the Tory party has moved light years in the course of thirty years, then the military has as well.

ANGELA EAGLE

The army has made enormous strides because you used to be dismissed if you came out but now they're actually recruiting young gay men and women. The transformation has been huge, including having a transsexual marine.

EVAN DAVIS

It was between 1998 and 1999 that the British newspapers flipped from projecting gay people as perverts and instead began to write about them in a way that was a little bit titillating, and interesting, and colourful. I don't know what caused that flip. It might have been David Yelland, the new editor of *The Sun* who was, I think, more socially liberal than some of his predecessors. It's helped change the social environment in a big way, especially amongst the young.

JASON PRINCE

Everything is so different now. When kids come out now they tell their mates at college and they all go out with a mixed group of guys and girls. They could be in Walkabout or they could be at G.A.Y, but really it's the same, they're just out with their mates and it's fantastic. It means everyone has become a little bit more liberal. Young people in general just aren't so hung up about what their sexuality is.

CHAPTER THIRTEEN

Setbacks

JULIAN CLARY

In 1993 I was the penultimate award of a long tedious *British Comedy Awards* live on TV. Norman Lamont, the much loathed chancellor of the exchequer, was in the audience and because the set was bedecked with foliage, I thought of a joke about how nice it was of them to make me feel at home by decorating it like Hampstead Heath. Then I said I'd just been fisting Norman Lamont backstage. It got a laugh and I thought – oh that's nice! But the next day the media called me foul-mouthed Clary and all my work dried up. Cancellations and no new bookings. I was in disgrace.

So I did what anyone would do in those circumstances, I went to Australia where you could talk about fisting on breakfast television. Which I did.

ZOE LYONS

Because the traditional view of a lesbian is that you were serious and slightly angry, you know, and because that was the only kind of people that used to be portrayed in films and plays, there is still a rather naive view among a lot of the less thoughtful parts of the audience that just assume any female comedian is a lesbian anyway, which I suppose takes some pressure of me. You know – she's clearly angry, she's got problems, she can't stop taking, she isn't happy with her life. So she's probably a lesbian. They just assume it, you know.

QBOY

Little Kim, Tupac, Snoop Doggy Dog, Foxy Brown, those were the people I was listening to in the midst of being bullied at school when everyone was calling me 'queer boy'. I came to terms with my sexuality and created a career for myself all in one go by creating the name QBoy, which was just an abbreviation what they were calling me anyway. I thought if I'm going to be an out queer hip hop artist then I'm not going to tone down my lyrics to please people, so a lot of my early stuff was really filthy, all about sex and cock and men. But most of the promoters at gay clubs didn't want to book me because I was a rapper. It's very narrow-minded – just because you like cock you're meant to listen to house music and take ecstasy.

MAJINDER SINGH SIDHU

I went to work for the UN in Palestine, it was very difficult because at that time I was going through depression and suicidal tenancies because I was in the closet, was living away from home, and wasn't talking to my family. We would go into detention centres next to the Egyptian border and interview people who had been tortured mutilated and had applied for UN protection. Some of them had been tortured because they were gay or lesbian. Many had been physically abused and raped multiple times, I mean machine guns put inside there vaginas or anuses, things like that, really horrifying things. We had to interview them. Some interviews I sat alone as a 24-year-old while someone cried for 4 hours continuously. It was very emotionally draining.

MATTHEW TODD

I think back to the Nineties when I was outside the House of Commons, you know, campaigning for the big visuals, like the age of consent. And all those people that were there trying to change things, everyone together. Then suddenly in bleak moments you see that we can be very aggressive and unpleasant towards each other. And that makes me very sad.

MANJINDER SINGH SIDHU

I went onto *Gay Romeo* when I was 18 or 19. I went onto profiles and so many profiles kept saying, "Muscular

masculine straight-acting white guy. No fems, no fats
no Asians, no blacks. Sorry this is not racism it's just my
preference." It's quite rampant

STEPHEN FRY

I'm always quite shocked if I meet a gay person who is
unsympathetic or racist. But of course, there are gay people
of all kinds, you know. Being born gay doesn't give you an
automatic membership of some guardian elitist society

MAJINDER SINGH SIDHU

I lived in Germany for a while and I was very fetishised. They
would touch my skin and say, "I love your skin colour, I love
the hair." But I didn't like it; I felt like a zoo animal.

MATTHEW TODD

I wrote my book *Straight Jacket* because even though I was
relatively successful, had written a play, was the editor of
Attitude, had met all these amazing celebrities and had an
exciting lifestyle, I still had a problem with self-esteem.

I was drinking too much and displayed some erratic
behaviour, and maybe sleeping with too many people. I'd seen
various therapists and councillors over the years and no one
had ever been able to help; no one had ever been able to make
things better; no one had ever been able to explain it. Then
a really good friend of mine who was on the verge of suicide
went into recovery and found a solution, a different way of
thinking about things, and I started to engage with that.

I met a gay therapist who said to me, "Well of course you're
fucked up, you're gay," which was a really confronting thing
for someone to say to me.

He went on to explain that it's not actually because you're
gay, it's because of what you have grown up with through
society invalidating you – you know, through homophobia

at school, religious institutions, the media – the whole experience.

LORD PADDICK

Unfortunately, there's still quite a lot of homophobia in the police service. Although I left in 2007, talking to colleagues who are still serving, there is still an undercurrent, it's the same as we found with sexism and racism, legislation tended to drive it underground rather than cure it. You could always tell when senior police officers stood at the front of the room extolling the virtues of diversity, who really meant it and who was just reading the words off the card.

LORD CASHMAN

We need to educate. It starts in the home, it's carried on in school, and the workplace. And where there are cultural attitudes that clash we need to work within those cultures and within those communities.

MATHEW TODD

I think it's very complicated when you come out. Growing up in the Eighties, I was told that gay people were all terrible and disgusting and horrible. Young people can be very aggressive. When I was working at Stonewall I remember going to some art college to give a talk and all the straight people were very receptive but two young gay people, who must have been 17 or 18, were really aggressive and said, 'You're making things worse. You're making straight people hate gay people.' I was representing Stonewall, a relatively conservative organization, so I think self-hatred can come through in very complicated ways.

ANGELA EAGLE

There's a lot of internationalization of hatred. In any generation there are some people who are very self-

confident, who can defy convention in that way, but I think
they're a minority, fantastic as they are. But a lot of people
internalise a lot of hatred and "*shame*" is the word that's
usually used.

MATTHEW TODD

I had a friend when I was younger who used to say: "I'm a
piece of shit and I will catch HIV because that's all I deserve."

And he did catch HIV – just a young guy who I knew years
ago when I first came out, around 17 or 18. There seemed to
be a lot of this kind of behavior based on shame, on low self-
esteem, about taking risks. And as a young gay man, when
Gaydar happened I was taking risks too. You know, it's not
particularity safe to constantly meet strangers online – but
it's something that's very common.

OLLY ALEXANDER

I have conversations with people about shame and I think
people sometimes take a different meaning from it to what I
think. It's hard because as gay people we are encouraged to
just be proud all the time, we have *Pride* every year, which is
super important, and I love being proud. But I guess pride is
the antithesis of shame. You can't always be proud of being
gay, nor can you always be ashamed.

MATTHEW TODD

Somewhere inside of me I still sometimes feel I'm not good
enough, and I still wrestle with it. I've certainly made lots
of progress and I feel far better than I ever have done, but
I know it's something that can still be there so I have to be
aware of it and on guard for it. It's like fighting a dragon when
it comes out of the cave. Previously I had no idea that there
was a dragon in the cave and I had no idea how to combat it.
Whereas at least I now do, and I've got some tools to help me.

SHON FAYE

Anyone who lived through the AIDS crisis will obviously think that things have improved, and they have, but there's a huge amount of ignorance. Some people will come out expect this to be the start of something positive because they've admitted who they are. But actually there are a lot of other circumstances – your class, your finances, your race, your religious background – all can still hold you back.

MATTHEW TODD

I was on *Gay Pride* marches feeling incredibly proud and consciously having no shame whatsoever, so it was bizarre that there was still this subconscious shame making me feel not very good about myself. It's a massive thing for a lot of LGBT people. We often don't feel safe and although we're in this period of change, a lot of people don't seem to be thriving.

JASON PRINCE

When the party scene was much bigger you know it was very hedonistic. You got the drug dealers, you got the porn stars, you got the rent boys, you got the DJs, and you got the drag queens, and they're all in hedonistic professions and having a great time. But you have to question who can actually be at *Heaven* at five o'clock on a Tuesday morning and be able to fit into any kind of normal life? There were still two thousand people in there every Tuesday morning at 5am when it closed and was time to go home. The gay scene attracted sheer hedonism. And there was bound to be a downside to that.

MATTHEW TODD

The traditional trajectory was – you struggle, you come out, you go into gay bars and you try and find a relationship.

But the gay interaction with consumerism and capitalism has complicated that because gay bars don't have the same feeling of being a place of sanctuary the way they did. There was a time when they really were the only place you could kind of relax and be yourself. Certainly, if you work in London there are probably other out gay people in the office and you probably have a lot of companies with decent policies about LGBT staff, so a gay bar is no longer the only place where can go and be yourself. I don't think it's as black and white as that anymore.

JASON PRINCE

I'm glad I got out while the going was good because I think it's turned a lot more into sex parties now. It's turned into a lot harder gear, and I'm pleased that I met Matt when I did, when it was still the fun party scene. There was always the availability of sex at bars or at parties but it wasn't just about that, you would still be in a group of friends having a great time and the boys were there if you wanted them. But it never seemed to be just about that.

Unfortunately, on the gay scene now, it's gone more into the saunas, or the sex parties, and away from the fun of the gay bars and clubs. I had fun times with it, but I'm pleased that I didn't get into the sex party scene.

MATTHEW TODD

Now the issue is chemsex parties. It's gotten a lot of attention over the last couple of years but it's been growing for the last decade. It's just a case of where people are going less to bars and clubs and are meeting up via apps like Grindr and Scruff to have house parties where people take drugs and have sex. What's not to like? I mean I can understand that totally, and I've written about it a lot in *Attitude*.

Sometimes people get into a defensive place where

everyone is being kind of judgmental and moralistic about it. But the fact is – these drugs are incredibly powerful and they kill lots of people. You know there are stories of people waking up and there is a dead body in the living room, I've lost count of the times I've heard about those kind of things.

QBOY

There are lots of different medications but most doctors try to put people on just one tablet a day and the one tablet will contain two or three different key ingredients. So, it's not just the apps and the websites that allow these young people to have these sex parties, or the cheap and readily available drugs like methadone and ketamine, it's also the thought in their head that, if I get HIV, if I become HIV positive, it's going to be fine, I'll just take a tablet every day.

But of course, that one tablet can give a lot of side effects.

JASON PRINCE

There was this lad who ran away from home when he was very young and moved to London, he'd just moved from Kent actually. But he found the whole experience of coming out as gay in this generation to be overwhelming, and he got involved very quickly with the drug scene, which affected him mentally.

He also contracted HIV, and the stigma that came with it caused him to try and kill himself. He threw himself in front of a train, which was just devastating for me, because I absolutely loved the lad. He lost both his legs and one of his arms. He was a very talented boy and he had a lot to live for.

He ended up in therapy and tried to get his life back as much as he could, but as soon as he had an opportunity he overdosed and succeeded in the end of killing himself. The regret that came with his suicide, I've never come to terms with.

MATTHEW TODD

There was a young man we interviewed for *Attitude* who said that after a party he was left high, literally high, on top of a multi-story block of flats just wandering around on the roof completely out of his head, and naked, because he was having a bad reaction to the drugs.

I think there's a lot of messy dangerous behaviour going on and it's really hard to talk about it because none of us want to be going, "Oh you shouldn't be doing this, you know."

I've taken drugs in the past, but not those drugs because they're just too dangerous. If we care about each other we need to have a discussion about it and just stop people dying. It would be a really good thing to happen.

SHON FAYE

I have gay male friends who started a sex life in their teens and a lot of them told me that they had unprotected sex and they exposed themselves to risk unknowingly for the first few years of their lives and I think that's very prevalent. It only takes a look on dating apps like Grindr or Scruff to see these men who you know they have 'discreet' on their profile because perhaps they are not living an openly gay life and they are essentially asking for condomless sex.

QBOY

Even now I meet young kids that are not very clued up or aware about HIV medication and treatment and they act like I acted when I was their age. They think that by having sex with someone who is open about their status that they are positive that's going to make them positive even though this positive person is on medication. So they avoid all those and then they go and have unprotected sex with someone whose status is completely unknown.

There are young people out there that are not really aware or conscious about their actions and how they are approaching this issue and how in the end it's probably going to lead to their own infection, which is a shame really because you think after all this time, all this education, all this information it's just not reaching the people it needs to reach. This is one of the reasons why the HIV rates are alarmingly high at the moment and keep rising

JASON PRINCE

What I've found is that even though the AIDS virus is under control with the medication that people can take, it's alright *if* they take it. But say you're a boy, and you have run away from home, and you've come from Liverpool to the lights of the big city. One of the first people you're probably going to meet is me, DJ-ing at *Fire* or singing at *Heaven*. I meet people quite often when they're first in London and I've seen the deterioration.

If a young lad like that catches HIV, even though there's no need for them to be ill if they can get it under control, the stigma is still there, and a lot of them go off the rails.

Suddenly they're at these sex parties, and they think they've got nothing to live for anymore. They get into heavy drugs and their life becomes shallow and meaningless to them.

It doesn't need to be like that, but I've seen it too many times now. Maybe it's the apps but I really don't know what the solution is.

MATTHEW TODD

Using an app is just so quick and easy isn't it. And if one has a problem with compulsive behavior, having Grindr is like an alcoholic having a beer pump in his pocket the whole time. It's just always there so you know at any time, any place, there is this constant kind of rejection, affirmation, rejection affirmation. It's very compulsive and if you have an issue with addiction – and that's a massive thing because that's what addiction is about, rejection, you know, highs and lows and so on so – I can see how that builds and makes people feel not very good about themselves.

You go onto Grindr and everyone looks absolutely gorgeous and stunning and like a porn star. You think, oh my God, how do I interact with this?

And people aren't very nice on apps – and I have done it too you know, I'm not perfect, I'm as much part of the issue myself.

By the way people are very abusive, you know... "Don't talk to me if you're like this." "Are you too feminine?" "Are you this? Are you that?"

JASON PRINCE

I think mental health is the worst it's ever been on the gay scene. It's not a physical thing like before with AIDS, I think now it's mental health. It's not having that backbone and structure, it's not having that social network that was there.

I think I was the last of the local pub generation. When I came out there were these wonderful older people I met. If I needed to, I could pick up the phone to them, if I had a problem.

Looking from a straight person's perceptive at the time, they probably would have thought, "Oh, dirty old man with a young lad." But it wasn't actually like that. The older queens looked after the younger queens.

Now, on Grindr now, you are probably never going to meet an older queen, because you'll just probably fancy boys your own age and never get to meet someone that might be there for you other than for a quick sexual encounter, or to make money. So, I find it very depressing.

STEPHEN K. AMOS

Parents will kick their children out for being gay and some young people end up homeless and vulnerable on the streets in a big city like Birmingham or Manchester or London, where they go into a life of whatever.

JASON PRINCE

At first I couldn't believe it, it was like a whole generation of boys whose first option was to go on the game. As a gay man I have got absolutely no moral objections about it at all, if that's what someone wants to do, but that's alright if they are older and adjusted enough mentally to be able to cope with the down side of it.

It's the mental state the boys get into nowadays. It's not having the support.

MATTHEW TODD

I begin my book with the story of somebody in our office who took his own life. He was the gay brother of a straight guy who'd worked in our office and had been there for a year. On the surface he ticked all the boxes of what it meant it be a happy successful gay man – he was attractive, he was sexually active on apps, and he had loads of friends on *Facebook*. He was real fun to be around and was laughing and joking and very confident – you'd think he didn't have a care in the world.

I didn't see him in a few years but I would speak to his brother who told me he'd become HIV positive and wasn't coping with it very well. He'd been the victim of several homophobic attacks and was drinking too much. He'd begun carrying lager with him in his rucksack as a kind of comfort so he knew that he had it with him.

At that point I was struggling with all my own stuff

so I wasn't in a position to help because I didn't really understand what was going on with my own life. But on the day that Margaret Thatcher died, he took his own life. It felt to me that there was a disproportionate number of gay people who were dying.

SHON FAYE

All LGBT people, trans people especially, have experienced higher rates of suicide, attempted suicide, mental health problems and abuse. It's quite astonishingly common and high among LGBT people, especially trans. The trouble is, from adolescence onwards we're looking to success stories – oh look, this person did it, and it's very impressive – though actually they must have worked a lot harder than sis gender heterosexual people might have. But whether or not it's good to have LGBT people in leading roles... Role models can actually be a side show for the fact that things don't improve overall.

LORD CASHMAN

We've changed the law but it's people being out that counts the most. More than anything we need role models – public figures being out, people in entertainment being out, footballers being out.

STEPHEN K. AMOS

If I was a professional footballer today, would I come out? I don't think I would if I wasn't sure what was going to happen with my family and inner circle of friends. It's OK being encouraged by your gay peers that you should do this but they don't live with it twenty-four seven. They don't know what the outcome is going to be, especially if you don't have that support network around. I can't imagine a seventeen-year-old trainee at *Manchester United* or *Chelsea* saying

"I'm gay" with all the stress that causes. But if a brilliant footballer, already successful at one of the biggest clubs in the world, chose to say it, he would influence a generation.

MARK McADAM

Many years ago, in 1990, Justin Fashanu came out as gay. An incredible guy with huge courage, but since then we've had decades of no one coming out.

PETER TATCHELL

When Justin Fashanu came out he was in the old First Division and it was not at all the ideal circumstances. My understanding is that he was going to be outed by *The Sun*. To forestall it, he offered them an exclusive story instead. He justified it on the grounds that they were going to publish anyway and that many of the most homophobic fans were readers of that newspaper, so I can sort of understand that.

The reaction of the black press was horrendous. He was disowned by his own brother, fellow footballer John Fashanu, and denounced in *The Voice* newspaper as bringing shame to the black community. That was an incredible blow and Justin was really proud of being black as well as being gay. He really identified and sought the support of the black community and to be stabbed in the back by his own brother and by the community's newspaper was a terrible blow. It brought him down really low.

TRIS PENNA

I used to go out with Justin Fashanu and I've written about how awfully he was treated by the heterosexual football establishment. Brian Clough in particular, who people still think of as a hero, wrote the most terrible things about him in his autobiography. Justin was bullied and made to feel less than worthless.

STEPHEN K. AMOS

The Fashanu story was very sad. I think, with the exemplary talents that he had as a professional footballer, one of the few black footballers at the time, it was terrible to have this burden on his shoulders, to be hiding something, which he felt he had to open up about.

PETER TATCHELL

I first met Justin at the gay nightclub *Heaven* in late 1981 before he came out. I was dancing and he was on the sidelines. He called me over and we began chatting. I had no idea who he was. He had no idea who I was. He had just become the first black footballer to get a million-pound transfer – from Norwich to Nottingham Forrest. I had just been selected as the labor candidate to fight the Bermondsey by-election. We kissed that night but that was it. We exchanged names and phone numbers and agreed to keep in touch.

After about six weeks we came out to each other, he learnt that I was a Labour candidate, I learnt that he was a footballer. He was very insecure about his sexuality. He was really struggling with his faith and his gayness. He was battling against the manager at Nottingham Forrest, Brian Clough, who was overtly homophobic. The conflict with Clough and his struggles to reconcile his faith with his sexuality ultimately led to declining performance on the pitch. He wasn't scoring the goals and it put him into a downward spiral. The more he thought about it the more depressed he got, and the more depressed he got the worse his game became. It was tragic to see his decline.

He would sometimes take me as his companion to family events and birthday parties often with other footballers. I can remember in late 1981 he was a judge at a black talent contest and he had me sit on his table on the stage in front of all the media. I was known to be gay and a champion of gay rights, and Justin was wearing a very flamboyant bright yellow tuxedo which should have set everyone's gaydar ringing. It was almost like he was begging to be outed – as if he was daring people to do it because he wanted to lift the burden. Yet he was never touched by the media in that period.

STEPHEN K. AMOS

Justin Fashanu was one of the few black footballers in the Football Association at that time, so he was a role model. And at the same time he was going through this inner turmoil of whether to come out or not and say he's gay. Then, when he does finally say it he gets rejection from his family and disapproval of his family and fans and friends. Suddenly he's left in the wilderness.

MARK McADAM

What makes the Justin Fashanu thing even sadder is that he was put in a situation where he felt he had to take his own life.

PETER TATCHELL

You could see him going down and down, and it was a tragedy. There was nothing that I or any other of his friends could do to help him. So when he finally killed himself, it was a shock, but something that felt almost destined to happen.

STEPHEN K. AMOS

I don't think the mainstream media realised just how heavy a burden it was. He tried to do something positive and it affected him in such a terrible detrimental way. He was left in the wilderness with all the struggles and mental torment, all the anguish which that puts on somebody. But of course, if it was possible I'd like to see every single *Premiership* footballer who is gay come out and say it. I do a lot of stuff for *Kick Homophobia out of Football* and there are a lot of players who support that initiative.

LORD CASHMAN

The sad thing is that homophobia and transphobia are now suddenly on the increase again. Hitting somebody because they are different has sadly come back into fashion in certain quarters, and we've got to be extremely vigilant. The social changes still need to be defended and advanced upon. The law signifies whether we are a civilised society or not, and the actions that people follow on the streets demonstrates whether that's really true or not.

STEPHEN K. AMOS

I also do work for a charity called the Albert Kennedy Trust which basically just deals with young vulnerable teenagers who've been kicked out of their family home.

ANGELA EAGLE

For kids who are thrown out of their family homes, that's really really tough. It's another reason why civil partnerships and gay marriage are so important. It normalises the relationships that gay people have and provides public recognition of them in a way that anyone who has any humanity can actually identify with.

LORD CASHMAN

The law has done all it can. The hate crime laws are there and there's greater power to sentence wrongdoers. But there simply isn't a political equation that can deal with homophobia and all the other phobias. Hate crimes still happen.

STEPHEN K. AMOS

Like the bombing at the Admiral Duncan pub. I used to

work with a guy who was actually there at the time the bomb went off. I remember it so clearly because that week there was also a bomb in Brixton market, then there was a bomb somewhere in the East End. It was very much a scare campaign for any minority. For someone like me, black and gay, you think, 'Oh my God, they've attacked my community twice now.' Then to have it happen so close to home with somebody I know.

I used to go to that pub myself and I remember clearly there was a front page picture in *The Guardian* where it's all dusty and smoky and there's somebody trying to climb out of the smoking ruin. That was my friend, and it's scarred him ever since. He's moved out of London, he's had to have counseling, in fact he wrote an amazing play about it.

That kind of atrocity brought different communities together. It showed there are people out there who see us all as deviants and that we should all be annihilated. Apart from spending years of having to fight for our own rights we're now being attacked. If that doesn't unify people then I don't know what does.

LORD CASHMAN

The bombing of The Admiral Duncan pub followed on quickly from two other bombings that had happened that weekend. I wasn't around the West End at the time, but the complete and utter sense of disbelief and the sense we thought we were through the worst that had happened to our community, through AIDS and HIV. I wouldn't say we were through it all, but through the worst, and then for this to happen was unimaginable and almost unbearable. But it brought about a political resolve, and a resolve within our community, that we should never suffer this again. That's where the LGBT communities have been different, we have never backed off from the challenge or from the threat. We have accepted it and said, 'OK, bring it on.'

CHAPTER FOURTEEN

Transitioning

PARIS LEES

You would have been more likely to have met an alien than a trans person in the mining town where I come from. Just growing up and realising that I am trans and thinking, 'Oh my God, I'm one of those people that are just ridiculed.'

STEPHANIE HIRST

My natural state of comfortableness is female. At school I was put with the boys and I distinctly remember looking over to the other side of the classroom and going – no, I should be over there, I shouldn't be with the boys.

That was at five years old but they didn't have a word for it then.

JAKE GRAF

I knew from pretty much as soon as I was aware of how everything worked around me that I was different, so probably when I was about two-and-a-half. You know all the little children run around naked on holiday and I knew I was missing something the other little boys had. They obviously pointed it out and I would feel wrong. My mother said I was quite an early talker and as soon as I could vocalise it, I'd say, 'I'm a boy,'

She'd say 'Oh don't be so silly.'

And I'd say, 'I'm a boy.'

This went on for years; struggling with being put into dresses on birthdays and at Christmas, and that sense of dread knowing it was going to happen.

For me this was a humiliation every time and it became a real problem because my mother and father, who were very loving and very caring, had no information back then about transgender, it simply wasn't discussed at all in the early Eighties. They really struggled with the fact they had this child who was adamant that he was a boy and refused to wear dresses. Or if he was bribed with a Mars bar would put a dress on for just half-an-hour to have a photo taken.

SHON FAYE

I was bullied and taunted at school for my effeminate behavior. I was raised Catholic and I was very religious throughout my teenage years. I became intensely religious when I was 14 which was probably a response to adolescence and the struggles I had with the start of puberty and sexual identity and gender. I was adamant I was going to become a Benedictine monk and I was considering applying for entry to a monastery and also possibly a legal career, but I ended up applying for an English degree. I'm not particularity religious now.

JAKE GRAF

Back in the Eighties there was no one else trans in the media, no one else trans on screen, and certainly if they were trans on screen they would have been the butt of the joke or the freak. I really felt I was the only person in the world that felt like that. It started so young that I didn't even realise the problem it was. I guess I used to pray that I'd wake up the next morning a boy and obviously that doesn't happen. It was a very difficult childhood of waiting and obviously becoming aware that puberty was going to hit at some point.

PARIS LEES

Mathew Todd writes brilliantly about the effect of growing up in the Eighties as a young gay boy reading headlines that called people names like poufter and realising at the age of 12 'I'm one of those people that are reviled' and I think that's very much true for trans people growing up too.

STEPHANIE HIRST

There was a picture of me taken at a radio station when I

was 12 years old and I'm leaning over the back of one of the DJ's and my T-shirt looks as if there is some kind of breast growth. I remember as a child staring at that picture every night, hoping and praying they were breasts, and they were growing, even though I knew they weren't.

JAKE GRAF

In my dreams I was always male and kissing girls, for instance, as a boy because I used to like girls and then waking up in the morning and realising it wasn't true, then going back to this feeling of 'Why am I the only one? Why must I be different?' It was very painful.

PARIS LEES

One of my earliest memories is sitting on a park bench with a girl and telling her that I'm a girl and her saying 'Oh! that's naughty,' and me thinking 'Oh God! what have I said?'

That was the first time I realised that the way that I saw myself wasn't the way that other people saw me. I was four when that happened.

JAKE GRAF

As puberty approached it was a feeling of absolute dread and again of doubling up on the prayers to some god that I would wake up and it would all be alright.

When puberty hit I did actually did start binding my chest and so on because that was something i couldn't deal with. I'd always liked girls from about three years old. I used to try and make friends with the girls in the playground. I had ridiculous crushes on them and I'd even tell my mum, 'I'm going to marry that one.'

I remember seeing Patsy Kensit as Cinderella on stage in the theatre. I must have been 11, and I told my mum I was going to marry Cinderella. Again she said, 'Don't be so silly darling.'

There was lots of 'Don't be so silly darling' in my childhood.

PARIS LEE

I was quite clear when I was a child that I was a girl. It was as simple to me as it was confusing to everybody else. But then of course you're told that's not possible, you can't be, you have a penis, you're a boy. That's it, end of. So you think – OK, well I'm a boy, and when you realise that you like boys you just think, well I'm one of those gay boys, because that's what it means.

It took me quite a few years to realise, no actually, I was right the first time, I'm a girl, this is possible, it's a thing, I can do this.

SHON FAYE

As a trans person I came through a gay identity first – I identified as a gay man for my early twenties.

I still think femininity is very demonised in a sexual way in the gay community. A drag queen may perform in drag, but probably if he's a gay man when he's trying to find sex he'll dress as a man. If you go to a gay club trying to meet people presenting yourself as feminine, that's something that's very marginalised. The gay community isn't above recreating the prejudices that are in society in general – there's definitely a lot of misogyny in the gay scene – a lot of attitudes about effeminate men embarrassing the community.

STEPHANIE HIRST

It's absolutely exhausting getting up every single day and knowing that you're not you're true self. You're not being yourself. As soon I said the words, "I'm transgender," my world came into focus. Colours seemed more vivid and everything stopped being a blur.

PARIS LEES

It's almost a cliché because it's quite common for trans people to remember that realising they saw themselves differently was one of their earliest memories. There's something quite fundamental about it.

It was when I hit puberty that I started to realise there were other people like me. I come from Nottingham, and in the Noughties I first started going clubbing in the city centre. As a 15-year-old, meeting people from all walks of life was a real eye opener. And then we had Nadia Romarda on *Big Brother* and that really changed it for me. I was like, 'Wow, this is an actual thing. I could do this. It's possible. Other people have done this and they're not freaks.'

JAKE GRAF

My parents always thought I was just a tomboy. I was very close to my father until puberty, we used to play tennis together and I was like his little chap – well, in my mind anyway – probably very different in his mind. I would do anything that he liked doing because it made me feel like being his boy. But I guess his perception was probably different.

PARIS LEES

Between 19 and 21 at university, I was desperate, suicidal, thinking – well there *are* other people like me, there's a word for people like me you know, so I can't be the only one struggling with this, there must be other people that are going through this.

Now of course we know that there are lots of people going through this all around the world. I was so suicidal and I was being treated so terribly just for being me. I remember being so desperate that I googled transgender people in the public eye, transgender people who were respected, though there were hardly any. I didn't find out about Jan Morris until a bit later but I came across Christine Burns and I saw that she had been honoured by the Queen. I thought – wow, that doesn't really fit with my idea of what a trans person is.

STEPHANIE HIRST

I went to my GP when I was 17 and was told to go away and think about it which I did for 20 years and then, yes, at thirty seven I decided that I can't do this, I'm doing a daily breakfast show broadcasting to well over one million people, I'm at the top of my professional game, I'm doing the national chart on a weekend. Literally, anything you could possibly want out of a radio career, I had. But I was trapped.

JAKE GRAF

I came out as a lesbian because I knew I liked girls and needed to find somewhere I belonged to get a sense of community. When I told a few friends I'd always felt like a boy, my best friend said, "Why don't you try the lesbian thing first?"

STEPHANIE HIRST

Do you know what it is? It's literally tits or death. Either you do it or you die. You get to a point where you can't survive because it's literally with you every single waking moment of your day from the moment you wake up to when you go to sleep at night.

JAKE GRAF

I became a very big part of the lesbian scene in London and worked in all the bars, Candy and so on. I was part of that scene for at least a decade; I'd found a community and was able to date. There were a lot of women that I guess were a lot like me and have probably since transitioned because obviously they were never really women. I knew that it was never right for me and it was a very destructive time in my life because as much as I became a part of the lesbian community there was always this feeling that men were the enemy, which is bizarre, but very common. So I felt out of place whilst still sort of being a part of this community.

PARIS LEES

I don't think trans people are confused at all, and if we've ever been confused it's because other people have made us so. I was watching an interesting lecture and one of the gender specialists working with kids was saying that gender dysphoria should be a pediatric issue, purely a pediatric issue, and I would agree with that. I mean the idea of people going to fake marriages because they don't want people to know that they're gay probably still happens but it feels incredibly old fashioned. I think the idea that people will get married, have kids and then come out as transgender in their forties is a shame. We need to support kids now so they don't have to go through an unwanted puberty – all that pain and trauma and hardship. I look at that and I think it's so unnecessary, it's avoidable, you look at the kids who are supported by their parents, who have got love. They're allowed to express themselves however they want to be – nobody is forcing them into surgery and they can put their puberty on pause and wait till they are a bit older and decide what they want to do. The overwhelming majority of them are happy and adjusted and able to lead normal healthy productive lives. Isn't that better than the stories we have heard from the older generation which is of just misery?

JAKE GRAF

Trans women are socialised as men. They therefore find it much easier to speak their minds. I think that's why there's such a huge trans female community, with clubs and bars and magazines, whereas trans men are a lot less visible and less vocal. We're socialised as women so we find it harder to find our voice because it's considered less important to hear a woman's perspective.

PARIS LEES

This whole feminist debate about whether trans women are really women is stupid. I just think, 'What are you even talking about?'

I'm lucky that I go about my daily business and people don't generally perceive me as being trans, or if they do they keep it to themselves. When I'm in shops and talking to people they call me miss, they refer to me with female pronouns, my boyfriend has never dated a transgender woman before and my family accepts me as female. If I worked in a shop I wouldn't ever think about the fact I was trans. I'm only trans when people remind me that I'm trans, or want to talk about it.

I know loads of kids who in their twenties had hormone blockers and went abroad for surgery quite young. They're supported by their families and they don't tell anyone that they're trans, or if they do it's not a big deal. There's no big coming out because they've always been who they've been from a young age.

I don't think my neighbours know that I am trans, I don't even know if the woman behind the reception in my doctor's surgery knows that I'm trans. You don't transition to be trans and of course more and more people are identifying as non-binary these days, which is great if that's what they want to do.

It comes down to that whole thing about labels doesn't it? People saying, 'Labels are for soup cans'. I think the whole thing about labels is that we choose out own, so labels can be great. I identify as a woman, nobody is forcing me to do that and I'm not forcing anyone else to identify as anything either. It's when people start forcing labels onto other people and say, 'You're this or you're that.' That's when it becomes a problem.

JAKE GRAF

There's a huge amount of segregation in the gay scene and today lesbians still go to one bar and gay men to another. The masculine gay men go to another bar and the queens to another. There's always been that divide.

In New York it was shocking when I was there in my twenties. It was one bar for the Latina lesbians, one bar for the black lesbians, and another for the white lesbians. And no one dared to cross those boundaries because it wouldn't have gone down well.

MATTHEW TODD

I think a lot of young people do care about the whole spectrum of the rainbow and all the different types of people that make up the whole family. It's been amazing to see awareness of transgender people come out of the shadows. I feel very sad when I see extreme feminists being really hostile to trans people. It completely doesn't make sense. It's tragic for us to become bullies of people like us – that's just not acceptable. That shouldn't be happening and there's no excuse for it.

ANGELA EAGLE

Somebody who bashes gay men is likely to have other prejudices too, you know – not liking women, having a thing about black people, or people with disabilities. If you have that kind of contempt for another human being it's likely to spread to other contexts. LGBT people have a lot in common with other groups that suffer some kind of bigotry, and the more we can make common cause the better.

TOM ROBINSON

You can't just fight for that one little group on its own while people with different colored skins are second class citizens, when a woman's place is in the home and you're just asking for equality for gay men. You've got to be a part of a much broader liberal agenda, trying to make the society more just.

PETER TATCHELL

The real breakthrough for trans people was in 2004 with the passage of the Gender Recognition Act. For the first time trans people were legally allowed to change their gender on official documents like passports. That was a really big change and it was the first of many subsequent legal reforms to protect trans people against discrimination in employment, housing and the provision of goods and services.

PARIS LEES

There's huge element of the abused abusing others, and it makes me really sad. We see it in the LGBT community where there are a lot of damaged people online. People who've experienced violence by men, people who've experienced violence in the streets or bullying at school. It can lead to lifelong physiological issues and it's really sad. This idea of the bitter self-loathing drag queen or older gay man is really sad and I just wonder, 'What did you go through that gave you all this hate in your heart?'

It's absolutely true that the bullied become the bully and I am an example of that. I was bullied really violently at school and I'm ashamed to say that I bullied other people as well. I don't think people go out and abuse other people if they're happy.

TOM ROBINSON

One of the ironies of my personal situation of being gay but also married with children, is that the queer basher doesn't care if you also fancy women; they're still going to kick your teeth down your throat for liking men.

SHON FAYE

There is a big divide between the rise of queer as a radical rejection of heterosexuals (and not fitting in with heterosexual society), and the campaign for gay marriage that is saying don't be afraid we are essentially just wanting the same institutions that you do – so that's the political side and then on the more personal side I think in the gay community because a trans person came through a gay identity first there is a lot of internalized homophobia that reflects the homophobia outside. I think it ties to the misogyny in society too and it's about being perceived as feminine and it is still much harder to be feminine, to be a woman in public life even if you just are a heterosexual woman, but particularly if you are perceived as a man who's acting like a woman. That's incredibly demonised because society still doesn't like, still doesn't like the idea that a man would resign maleness and behave effeminately. I think there is a bigger gap now as well because early on there was a gap between transsexuals and transvestites and a lot of them were drag queens as well, now most of the drag queens I know are men and they live their lives as men, they don't present like me on a daily basis.

JAKE GRAF

When *Boys Don't Cry* came out it was the first time that a trans man was represented in an even slightly sympathetic way on screen. But it was a horrific film because the trans character had been raped and shot. A really miserable story.

Boys Don't Cry was the story of a trans man called Brandan Tina who left his small town in middle America and went to a new town and presented as male. He didn't have hormones because they weren't available but managed to present as male and befriended a young girl and her older brothers and actually started dating this girl. Whether or not she actually knew that he was genetically female or not is not clear but at some point her brothers find out that Brandon had been passing himself off as a genetic male and take him out to a field and rape him, and eventually, as an upshot of that he's shot. He was played by Hilary Swank who played this trans male role quite well.

MATTHEW TODD

I think there is a whole group of young people who are, in a good way, not respecting the rules that have been set by the older generation. I think it's great for them to set their own narratives because it's up to them to define their own lives and their experience in the way they want to. I think that can be quite difficult for older people and sometimes it can feel really boring. I think it's really exciting this idea of breaking out of the binary of gender. I think probably a lot more people would have done that if it had been possible. For my generation it felt like we were there campaigning for all the different rights, which was a really important thing to do, but maybe now there's a bit more space to kind of think about how I want to express myself with regard to gender and clothes.

PARIS LEES

For me the biggest things to happen was Nadia Romada winning *Big Brother* because it was a trans person winning what is essentially a popularity contest. It turned everything I thought I knew about trans people completely on its head.

I just thought it was a life of misery with people being disgusted with you and I would have to be lonely, but there she was having a laugh and crying about cigarettes and getting involved with drama and doing all the things that the other house mates were doing. So as a young teenager watching that I was like, wow, OK, so I can just be me.

That's why media representation is so important, because if you don't know a trans person then what are you basing your information about trans people on?

That was the first time that I'd seen someone like that and fast forward ten years and trans people are absolutely everywhere, it's it fantastic. I didn't think it would become so inspirational but if you look around you there are trans people in modeling, gracing the cover of magazines, winning awards. I mean this is a new world. This just wasn't the world I was born into!

JAKE GRAF

It was a couple of years after *Boys Don't Cry* that I moved to New York for a year, and when you're gay and you move anywhere in the world you find your community – you find your bar and you find friends quite easily.

My straight friends are jealous of this. But when I went into the US lesbian scene there was this young really cute, really sort of handsome little guy and I wondered why he was always around and why the women were so welcoming and supportive of him. After a couple of weeks of chatting to this guy, Nico, he told me that he was trans, and I was obviously totally bowled over by a really handsome, really sweet, lovely guy who was living a very happy life designing furniture and doing very well. That was the first time I realised there was hope and that people could live happy, normal, trans lives. So I came back from New York and told my mum, and about four months after that I was starting testosterone and having top surgery.

BARONESS BARKER

Nobody talked about non-binary when I was young. I had no idea what it meant, but I'm beginning to understand it now. I'm beginning to have really interesting conversations about how there are all sorts of people that LGBTI includes. We do all get lumped together and it's good that we should support each other because we've still got a lot of battles to face and solidarity is important. But we're very different and I am pleased we've got to a point where we can be much more open as a community about the differences that we have. The issues for trans people are different to the issues for me, but that doesn't stop me trying to learn about it and be supportive, and to expect the same in return.

MATTHEW TODD

Well it's interesting isn't it that there's been an explosion in the number of people wanting to go through gender therapy or gender reassignment. It's really interesting because there used to be a narrative that you could only be trans if you were completely aware that you were trans from the age of five and you'd always known it was something you had to do.

I meet more and more people now who have lived as gay men or lesbians and have decided in their twenties, thirties, or sometimes forties, that they want to transition. I think it's a positive thing that people are more relaxed, that people feel they can go down that route if they want to. I guess with this whole queer and non-binary thing that has evolved we have this narrative that we're free and easy and we don't put people into boxes, people can be whoever they are and not feel the need to put a label on it.

When you talk about identity with gay men they're

obsessed with labels, be it top, bottom, twink, bear, this, that, you. There's still a strong vain of campness, or whatever you want to call it. Younger people really identify with things like *Ru Paul's Drag Race*. I see so much passion for the drag queens on that show, and the use of that method of finding out who you are – through fashion, and quipping, and lip-syncing and entertainment!

SHON FAYE

But you know there are mental health tolls with transition. I've had severe mental health problems in my life, throughout my life, and through my adolescence.

PARIS LEES

I don't think I know a single trans person who doesn't suffer greatly in private. I have days where I throw my hands up and feel like I can't go on – like it's too much – I'm incredibly privileged. If you're 15 years old and living on a rough estate in Manchester and your father's homophobic and you've got a pretty good idea that he won't accept you being a different gender, you're not going to be benefiting from this transgender tipping point. That not to dismiss the great gains being made because they're all important parts of the process and it would have made a huge difference to me to actually see trans people celebrated in the culture when I was growing up.

Being taken seriously, being respected that would have sent the message to me that I'm OK, and that if anyone has a problem with me then that's their problem. I didn't get that message until much later in my life – but for many trans people in England it's still the dark old days.

JAKE GRAF

My father died when I was 18, so he never knew about any

of it, never knew about me as a lesbian, never knew about trans. When I came out as a lesbian my mother was quite supportive and said "as long as you're happy." Then, years later when I came out as trans she said was "Okay what are we going to do about this?" So that was lovely.

But strangely enough, when I reminded her of the fact that I'd always felt I was a boy, she said "Oh! I remember you used to be a tom boy."

I said "No! Don't you remember?"

So she dug out all the old cards I'd written – Fathers Day cards, Mothers Day cards, birthday cards over the years, and I would sign them all with variations of my female name but with sort of you know Charles or Mark or Steve or Frank added onto the beginning. So she had all these cards and I said, "Didn't this give you any inkling?"

"Well no darling, I thought you were just a tom boy." So there you go!

She was very supportive and helped me through the surgeries and the hormones and through everything else, and brought me McDonald's after my top surgery and has been great to this day.

My father was a French jew and his parents died in the holocaust. He ran a wig and makeup company called Wig Creations over here and I went to the French Lycée in South Kensington for 13 years, so it was a privileged childhood. He never knew his parents because he was six months old when they were taken, he was raised in the French countryside as Catholic by his uncle so he wouldn't hopefully at any point ever be at risk again, he'd always kept his faith but we certainly weren't a Jewish family by any means.

My experience of Jewish families is by shaped by my experience of this guy called Simon outside G.A.Y about ten years ago. He was a Hasidic Jew and just used to stand outside every Friday night and watch everyone come and go. I would go and talk to him every week and say "Why don't you just come in?"

He said, "No I can't. If I walk through the door my family won't talk to me anymore. I know that's the only way I am going to be happy, but I can't."

Then one day he just wasn't there anymore and whether or not he ever came out I don't know. Whether or not my father would have been accepting is anyone's guess. My mother has been fabulous.

PARIS LEES

I have friends who don't blend in as well me and who are perceived as transgender. When they walk down the street they face abuse on a daily basis. How can we say things are better if it's still not OK to walk down the street and be trans? People say we've got gay marriage now but if people don't feel safe to walk down the street and simply be themselves how can we possibly say that we've reached where we need to be? That is not a civilised society if people are in fear of walking out of their front door. I don't know a single trans person who hasn't laid in bed and looked up at the ceiling and thought – I don't know if I can do this today, I just don't know if I'm strong enough.

That might sound melodramatic but I think it's the reality for many of us – and that includes me.

JAKE GRAF

Because, before *Boys Don't Cry*, I was such a part of the lesbian scene, I tried to accept my lot that I was going to be living as a woman and that's as far as I would ever get, but and obviously it wasn't a happy lot and very alcohol fuelled. As a result I remember the first lesbian kiss on Brookside which was Anna Friel in the soap kissing the ginger nanny, Margaret. It was a major thing and I used to sneak up to my mum's bedroom where we had all the compilation tapes and I would sit there just going record, stop, record, stop, so eventually I could watch just hours of Anna Friel being a lesbian, who also murdered her father and stuck him under the patio. (Lesbians are often portrayed as murderers, either getting bumped off or bumping other people off.)

ANGELA EAGLE

Of course, trans rights are behind in law and there are some issues around marriage and gender reassignment that we still have to think about. There are some very vibrant debates about how to absorb some of the issues that being trans throws up.

PARIS LEES

I'm not really that political to be honest. Where I come from we just didn't get involved with politics. No one told us that our opinions mattered and it's interesting really because if I hadn't seen the way that trans people were completely humiliated and lied about for decades then I probably wouldn't have become politicised. It made me look at the way power is distributed in Britain and the way the establishment gets away with treating minorities.

JAKE GRAF

There are so many different parts of the spectrum. I don't think anyone is a *real* man or a *real* woman. You know, there are men that I look at and think -oh for God's sake, be a man, which is a terrible thing for me to admit. I think – oh you're so camp!

By the same token there are women who are women who are born female who look incredibly masculine yet are totally straight. It's very much in your head as opposed to your body.

STEPHANIE HIRST

Because I'm a broadcaster, and especially on radio, one makes a decision on somebody's gender immediately through what you hear. So I didn't want the listener to hear someone that sounded remotely male. I worked really hard on it. My voice was the one thing that worried me the most in transitioning. Once I had pushed the button and said, "Right, I'm going to do this," the voice was the next important thing, because it's my tool. I need it to be able to communicate. There are some people I know who are trans and unfortunately just the way their voice box is built it doesn't allow them to be able to feminise it as well as other people can. There are countries where you can have vocal surgery and it does work, but you can't speak for two or three months and there is a risk. As a broadcaster you just know that if something was to go wrong you'd be mortified.

ANGELA EAGLE

There is 'Q' and 'I' and all sorts now and that's their choice. They have to navigate through their lives in the way they want. I remember talking to Ellen DeGeneres's mother at some *Channel 4* event and she said to me that, once Ellen came out, all of a sudden she wasn't the right sort of lesbian.

JAKE GRAF

In all fairness, I do feel more comfortable going into the men's toilet knowing there aren't women in there listening to you. And by the same token I don't feel that women should have to walk into a men's toilet and smell that absolutely awful smell that's very much associated with men. Women like to flower it up and put on a bit of powder and you know enjoy themselves in the loo, and chat. Men like to go in and do a totally different thing. At the same time, there are a boys that like to go in and put on a bit of makeup and women that want to wee.

I was at Channel 4 the other day and they have a gender neutral toilet. I thought how wonderful that you're all together, but weirdly they still put men and women stickers on the different cubicles, which seems totally pointless.

ANGELA EAGLE

We should stop being so judgmental. People have got to find their own way through their own identities, and navigate their lives without people standing by metaphorically with their hands on their hips saying, "Well, you're not doing that the proper way!"

JAKE GRAF

I shot *X-Why* over two years using my own transition to illustrate the story of the character in the film transitioning. What took two years in real life took just 17 minutes onscreen, so quite suddenly, you know, I had a beard, and suddenly I had muscles, and suddenly my voice had dropped, none of which had been done before in a film, so that did quite well. Then I made *Brace* which has been to about 80 film festivals across the world and was about two gay trans guys. Interestingly, a lot of trans men end up becoming gay trans men having always previously been attracted only to women. And after about six months on testosterone I found myself very attracted to men in an almost all-encompassing way. I mean it was hard, it was a real, "Oh my God! Now I not only have to re-adjust to society and friends and family and everyone else, and how they perceive me, but I have to rethink my whole identity."

SHON FAYE

I still think there's a shared LGBT community and I still consider myself to be a part of it – or you could put a Q on the end if you want. My identity has changed even though I've always described myself as Queer – but I used to let people think I was a gay man and then began to transition. I'm a trans person now so I've changed letters but I still feel it's important to have that shared community and I'm still friends with a lot of gay men. I can understand you can still see LGBT as a community yet see acute divides within that community. UKIP wanted to march at pride in London a year or two back and there was a huge debate about whether or not they should be allowed. Some people felt it was more inclusive to have a fascist party marching in pride while many black and minority ethnic LGBT people said, "This is unacceptable, these people are xenophobes, racists and you're excluding us by including them."

JAKE GRAF

I would be out in bars and there are always guys and it's weird how gay men can spot other gay men. So I dated a couple of guys, I dated one guys for six months actually, a very sweet guy and then I realised that if anything I still liked girls as well and this has just sort of broadened my horizons. I was attracted to men and women and now I'm dating a trans woman – Captain Hannah Winterbourne, who is the highest ranking transgender officer in the British army.

PARIS LEES

It frustrates me that LGBT people suffer such high levels of discrimination because it's completely unnecessary. Trans people have existed in every recorded culture around the world throughout history. The only thing that has changed is the way that other people within those societies have treated us. We haven't changed; it's other people.

SHON FAYE

Legal rights for transgender people in Pakistan are moving more quickly than gay rights and I think in Europe and America there was a stage in the early Seventies where transsexuals and the gay movement did both consider disconnecting. The gay movement won that because transsexuals still had to deal with the medical establishment. I have to go and engage with doctors in order to take hormones and until the AIDS crisis, at least, there wasn't that kind of relationship with doctors. So in the west it was easier for the gay movement to move along and now trans people are catching up.

There is also an overlap between transsexuals and fem gay men. They are covered now by labels such as gender queer and non-binary. I have a couple of friends who would describe themselves as gender queer who present as quite androgynous but were signed male at birth and have sex with gay men – but they don't see themselves as men or women. They see themselves as something else and they live their lives like that.

I think there will always be those people, and they'll often be referred to as gay, and it's interesting that there's this move to new labels because the old ones have changed or narrowed in meaning and they don't feel they fit that identity any more.

JAKE GRAF

At this point there's still a lot of broadening of minds and perspectives that film can really bring about. One of my films *Chance* was about two older, slightly larger, gay men, one of who was a widow and one who was a Muslim, and they meet and fall in love. It did very well because again people had never seen this on screen.

My most recent film *Dusk* deals with an older trans person who never had the chance to medically transition. These are all stories that people haven't seen and I think it's important that these stories are getting told. These aren't my stories any more, being used as a kind of catharsis, now I'm writing purely stories that people have told me, characters that I think, 'well, I've never seen you on screen, certainly somebody should be telling your story.'

SHON FAYE

There's a divide between the friends of mine who are gay men, who usually went to a private school and Oxford, who all have jobs in London and live with their boyfriends or partners, and my friends who are queer and have more radical politics. A lot of them are trans or gender non-conforming in some way. They also tend to be from a working-class background and be in the arts or media and not well paid. I think there's an ideological divide now around the idea of being hetro normative, trying to behave like heterosexuals. There's the idea that there is a homo-normative way to act and you have to rebel against that.

JAKE GRAF

Having found that I have an attraction to gay men I guess has made me more interested in that. *Brace* was very much my story at the time – but you know I had then met a girl who I was very much in love with, and then my attractions shifted and I had to leave her. It was what had just happened to me and then i was doing it to someone else, which didn't sit terribly well. Then I became a part of the gay male scene, so that was the story and that was why I wrote *Brace*.

I wrote *Chance* because I spoke to an older friend of mine

who is about 45 and said, "You know once you're thirty you're literally invisible on the gay scene," and he was a larger guy, about 18 stone

I wanted to write his story and I had another friend who is a Muslim guy, a Saudi man, a Saudi prince strangely enough, who I think is gay though he denies it vehemently. I just thought they'd make a beautiful union.

They were very open to this film which again pounded the festival circuit and got picked up by the British Film Council. People keep saying I'll have to move away from queer and LGBT stories at some point because otherwise I'll always be pigeonholed as the a queer, trans, LGBT writer, actor, director. But i think at the moment there are so many stories that need to be told that what I have done is write an eight-part web series called *Spectrum* which attempts to normalise the trans and queer experience.

PARIS LEES

If society was a bit more relaxed around gender I think there would be quite a number of trans people who wouldn't feel the need to transition totally from A to B. For other people it's quite a binary thing, a physical problem just like if you had an extra toe that needed removing. You know what gender you really are and you need an operation to put things right.

Transgender covers a broad group of people and for many of them it's very important to be physically in line with how they feel inside. For me, this is how I express myself. I'm not trying to be a woman, I just know that being perceived as a woman makes me feel happier. I don't know why; I don't need a scientific theory; I don't need an academic theory; I don't need a political theory; I don't need a justification, but this is how I am.

I'm not hurting anybody and if I want to call myself a woman then I am one.

JAKE GRAF

For me, a trans woman is totally a woman and a trans man is totally a man if that's how he feels and defines himself.

PARIS LEES

I really try to practice gratitude, just for my mental health more than anything. I'm just so happy to be here and to be healthy because so many trans and LGBT people don't make it through.

CHAPTER FIFTEEN

Gay marriage

ZOE LYONS

My wife is incredibly supportive. She's seen enough comedy and been around with me enough to know what it's like, what a roller coaster it can be, and she's great. She'll just says, "It happens. You'll get over it. You'll be fine."

She doesn't indulge me too much.

TOM ROBINSON

There is a musician I've known for the last 20 years from a tough part of Manchester and I'd worked with him for about four years when he suddenly and totally unexpectedly came out to me. You could have knocked me over with a rolling pin with the idea that this extraordinary macho man was actually gay and had been hiding it for thirty years. He eventually met the love of his life and had a civil partnership in the mid-Noughties and what was amazing was that he had feared for his life growing up in Moss Side, worried about what people would think of him if they ever knew he was gay. For thirty years he'd been in terror of that but once he'd fallen in love he decided love conquers all and arranged the civil partnership with his family coming down en masse. Grandparents, little kids, the entire tribe, everybody came down to Islington registry office and then to the party afterwards.

It was the most joyous, wonderful, celebratory thing and it just showed that if you come out and you're honest enough and you live openly, then people who you think might disapprove – who might have said homophobic things in your hearing – when they find out that you're one of those people, they change their minds about what those people are. They realise it's their brother, it's their son, it's their best friend and that's what gives us gay liberation. That's what has brought us as far as we are. It was the most life affirming thing seeing those Mancunian grandparents and the five year olds running around at the party afterwards and these two men in their suits blissfully happy together.

ANGELA EAGLE

The acceptance of civil partnerships and gay marriage is so important because it normalises the relationships that gay people have and it provides a public recognition in a way that anyone who's got any humanity can actually identify with. I think it has been an enormous civilising influence. I was brought up by my mum and dad to be very confident in my own abilities. They would never have had a problem with me being gay. My dad didn't have a problem with it, but I never formally came out to my mum. She died when I was 25 and I hadn't come out then, but she knew, and she was very supportive of all her children. So, I never had a problem at home.

PETER TATCHELL

The campaign for gay marriage began way back in 1992 when Outrage organised five same-sex couples to file applications for a marriage license at Westminster registry office. They were, of course, refused but that was the opening shot in the battle for same-sex marriage. The endeavor was renewed in 2010 with the formation of the equal love campaign to overturn the twin bans – the ban on heterosexual couples having a civil partnership and the ban on gay couples having a civil marriage. We wanted equality in civil partnership and civil marriage law for everyone. The campaign resulted in an application to the European Court of Human Rights in 2011 where four same-sex couples and four opposite-sex couples filed applications to overturn the ban on straight civil partnerships and the ban on gay civil marriages.

BARONESS BARKER

This summer, after 28 years together, we got married. It was the most wonderful day with our families and friends. There's a fair amount of pressure when you get married after having been together for 28 years. A lot of people said, "Why are you doing this?"

The simple answer was, "We wanted to in the past, but we couldn't. Now we can, so we will.'"

It wasn't about our relationship, it was about something altogether different. It's hugely important and symbolic. This is about LGBT people being celebrated in communities and families, and about being accorded dignity. It's not about frocks and cakes and all of that, it's about having a day on which your relationship is celebrated as equal.

PETER TATCHELL

Soon after he was elected mayor Boris Johnson attended London LGBT pride. I ambushed him in front of the national media to ask him if he would support the campaign for equal marriage. He was flustered but eventually said yes.

Once we got Boris Johnson to publicly support same sex marriage we used his support as leverage to get Tory MPs to follow suit. We also had the case against the ban on same sex marriage which we had bought in the European court of human rights. We said to David Cameron's advisers, "You don't want the European court to rule and force you to act. Why not take the moral high ground and use this as a way of showing your liberal credentials."

So that's ultimately how same sex marriage came to be.

MANJINDER SINGH SIDHU

When marriage was legalised in the UK that was a good thing because I've always wanted to get married to my partner and now we have gay marriage. The US and Ireland also have gay marriage and these are countries you would never have thought would do it, so it gave me hope because I thought if they can do it there maybe we can do it in India too.

At this point in history the West is doing these things more progressively than the East though this wasn't always the case. Back in the day in India it was OK to be gay, and if we can overturn the colonial laws that discriminate against gay people I would love to be one of the first people to be legally married in India. That would be a wonderful dream.

DEREK JACOBI

We had a civil ceremony but we haven't had the marriage yet. When we became civil partners there were about 25 people there and very curiously at one stage we were looking around and there wasn't a single gay person in the room. It was rather wonderful that somehow all our nearest and dearest were straight.

I'd got to the age of 39 not having lived with anybody. I'd had affairs but I was very set in my ways. Then I met somebody who was 17 years younger than me and it all happened, and that was 40 years ago. He was in the same business and profession and in the same company and there were tricky moments with hotels and that sort of thing and we had to be discreet. It all became easier when to be gay was no longer a big deal.

MATTHEW PARRIS

I'm all for civil partnerships, and I'm all for equal marriage, but I think it would be a pity if we moved into an era and a generation who, just like the straight side of the equation, felt the first thing you had to do was get a partner and be with somebody all the time. I would like gay culture to be tolerant of a wider range of attitudes than that.

I went through the whole civil ceremony bit, but those things don't really mean much to me. The tax advantage of having a civil partnership certainly meant something to me, because I'd be able to leave everything to Julian, without tax being paid. But as for the vows and that kind of thing, I just don't care for that. It's as though the state has defined a one-size-fits-all relationship and you walk into it. That's the relationship you wear, and there aren't any others. I really hope being gay is going to encompass a wide range of different friendships and partnerships that people can have.

MATT LUCAS

As gay people, we don't really have a template in terms of what a relationship looks like. Now marriage has been legalised, is it right for us to assume, and for other people to assume, that gay relationships will take the form of straight relationships? I think is a bit naïve, frankly.

We've always had to hide and find other pathways to love. I don't know any straight people who sit down on the first date and say, "Oh, are you looking for a monogamous relationship or an open relationship?" I mean, none of my straight friends do that. They're kind of shocked if I tell them those are the kind of conversations gay people often have.

MATTHEW PARRIS

Those who supported *Section 28* did so in an unpleasantly right-wing, morally conservative, sort of way – rather like, many years later, the gay marriage issue. It was another thing I didn't feel too strongly about one way or another, but nevertheless it defined which side you had to be on.

MATT LUCAS

There was a lot of judgment a year or so back of a famous

gay couple, whom the press weren't allowed to name, but who have an open relationship. The press saw this as hypocritical because the couple had had quite a high-profile wedding. My response to that was – you've spent years denying us love, you've spent years not legitimising our love, and, now we have equal marriage rights. It's not for the straight media to decide what a gay marriage is – don't assume that our relationships are monogamous and conventional. Many of them are, I've been in a really happy monogamous relationship, but you don't know what's going on in a gay marriage. Don't assume that an open relationship is an unhappy relationship, or non-consensual, or any of that. We've had to find different pathways to love and affection, we've had to find it where we can. It's been in stolen moments with different people, sometimes more than we want it to be, because the notion of falling in love with another man has terrified straight people over the years. I don't think straight people ever truly had a massive problem with two men having sex with each other – the big fear was two men being in love with each other.

MATTHEW PARRIS

I never believed that life, or sex, or sexuality should be looked at in terms of exclusively, or the search for a monogamous lifetime partner. I think romance can be overdone, and I think monogamy can be overdone too. Walking around arm in arm with a partner all your life can feel like you are having to lean on somebody, and I never wanted to lean on anybody, and I didn't really want anybody to lean on me.

So I was never a great one for arguing that everyone should be married, just like straight people. In the end it just sort of happened to me, and it's very nice. I love my partner and he loves me, and it's a monogamous relationship. But I hesitate to preach that this is what everybody should have. I'm entirely aware that if I was on my own I would still be happy, and I would still have friends. It's perfectly OK to be an ageing gay man who doesn't have a partner and has a wonderful social life.

PARIS LEES

How are we going to work together as a human race if we're still bickering and squabbling over who people can have sex with, or fall in love with, or marry? This has been an interesting moment in history, but more importantly we need to accept people for who they are and focus on the things that really threaten all of us. I'm not just saying it because it sound good. It's just ridiculous that we waste so much time like this.

MATT LUCAS

My marriage is a hard thing for me to talk about because we were married and my partner had an addiction. Then we separated, and he killed himself. He and I had an agreement that we would never really discuss those things publicly, so it's a hard thing for me to do. We had a civil partnership many years ago and I asked the registrar before the big day, what the difference was legally between a civil partnership and a marriage. He said they were the same thing, except you can't mention God in a civil partnership.

I said, "What, you can't even say, 'Oh God, I'm gay, and I'm marrying a man'"?

PARIS LEES

We need to progress from this medieval mindset – it's our lizard brains isn't it? It's that older part of us that's based on fear, passion, anger, and not on logical reasoning. It genuinely worries me. The world is a really volatile place at the moment and people are still tied up with such pettiness.

SHON FAYE

Teresa May said last year she didn't like gay marriage, yet for the previous four years the Tories had really been trying to see themselves as an ally for LGBT people despite being full of people who implemented *Section 28*.

STEPHEN K. AMOS

I love the way Wanda Sykes is uncompromising in her stand up when she talks about her marriage to her wife. She talks about their kids and I think that's so honest and real when she could just have been talking about rap music or whatever. But she has chosen to use that platform in such a positive way.

REVEREND ANDREW FORESHEW-CAIN

When I got married in 2014 I was disciplined by the *Church of England*, I was given what they called 'an informal rebuke', which actually doesn't exist. The *Church of England* doesn't have any official structures other than the *Clergy Discipline Measure*, and the 'informal rebuke' doesn't actually exist within the clergy discipline measure. So they made something up as a convenient way of sort of slapping me on the wrist. But of course the *Church of England* is very good at saying one thing and doing something else. I'd only been disciplined, but there were a whole bunch of consequences that came with that. They weren't articulated but they slowly become apparent. I'll never be allowed to move from my current job because I'll never be re-licensed in another job. I'm not allowed to have a curate to train because I'm no longer thought to be a suitable person to train another priest. I'm not allowed to be given any kind of acknowledgment. or preferment, or authority within the church.

STEPHEN K. AMOS

If I was a law maker, and my son or my daughter was gay, and I knew that they couldn't legally marry the person they were in love with, and therefore couldn't have any legal redress in case anything happened, I would do something about it. I would have to, that's just being human.

How can you look your child in they eye and go, "We're not going to pass this law."

REVEREND ANDREW FORESHEW-CAIN

When I was selected to be a priest everybody in my section knew I was gay and one of my selectors was gay and was quite open about it. And back in the Eightiesie before the church began to get timid and scared, the church was actually quite a safe place for gay people. 'Don't ask don't tell', which was kind of the rule in wider society was also the rule in the church, and there was a lot of understanding and acceptance of gay people as long as you were discreet. There were no questions asked of my sexuality in the way that are asked nowadays of people who want to be priests.

I'd been with my partner Steven for a very long time. In 2014, because same sex marriage was coming in, I asked him to marry me on Valentines day, and he said, "Yes!"

I tweeted it to my friends and the next day the bishops published their pastoral letter, later called the *Valentines Day Massacre*. It basically said, "Gay clergy are not allowed to get married and if you do we'll discipline you."

In fact, legally, gay clergy can get married if they really must though it's not what the bishops want. But because I'd tweeted that I was getting engaged and a couple of journalist had picked it up, it blew into a big story

TRIS PENNA

To be honest, I would make all marriage illegal. That would be my approach on equality.

But since I believe in equality, and we still don't have it, what's playing out is quite interesting in terms of religion versus gay people.

REVEREND ANDREW FORESHEW-CAIN

In the *Church of England*, the evangelical movement that grew up in the Sixties has grown in strength and contains within in it people who are viscerally against gay and lesbian people. The *Church of England* has produced various responses to the changing attitude towards sexuality and trying to find a way forward with regard to equal marriage, which became law in 2014, it was recommended that the church should *not* allow services of blessing. It shouldn't change its teaching. But it could offer informal prayers to gay and lesbian couples who want to get married – and do that in church.

But it went on to say that the couple who wanted that should at the same time be slightly told off because they were breaking the church's teaching. They were supposed to be told, "You're going against the official teaching of the church."

When they come in to see the vicar and say, "We're getting married next month and we would love to have the church recognise it," the vicar is supposed to reply, "How lovely for you, but although we're against homophobia in this church, we won't be able to recognise your marriage or bless it. However, if you want to, you can have some informal prayers in my study. But please do realise, we think what you're doing is terribly wrong."

That was what was recommended.

STEPHEN K. AMOS

Before civil partnerships, gay couples were so badly treated. I've heard so many horror stories of the family of a partner who dies taking away all their possessions and organising the funeral, telling his or her partner of 5, 10 or 15 years that they have no rights. Everyone chooses who they love, and the person who they love has got to be the one who makes those decisions with them. How can they can't be left in the air like that at a time when they're having to deal with the loss of their partner. I can't believe that in Australia they were still debating gay marriage last year. Even South Africa has now got gay marriage.

REVEREND ANDREW FORESHEW-CAIN

I went to Royal Festival Hall in 2014 and Sandy Toksvig and her partner were renewing their vows to each other, which they did in in front of 4,000 people. I sat in this hall with my husband, and it was when we were planning our marriage. We looked around and there were all these older couples who'd been together for a very long time celebrating the love that another couple had found in each other, and doing it with such generosity and spirit. It significantly increased my determination to resist the pressure being put on me not to get married.

YOTAN OTTOLENGHI

In my experience, the public are generally more open than we give them credit for. Though I had had a lot of worries about it, I've never experienced any negative reactions to us being two men with children. I used to think, "What are people going to say?"

We're all carrying those hang-ups with us in all sorts of fields, and parenting is just one of them.

BARONESS BARKER

In 2002 the then Blair government put forward the *Children Adoption Act*. It was the first recognition that families could come in a lot of different shapes and sizes. It was interesting because what the government was proposing was that adoption should be possible for people who were single, or who were not married, or for same sex couples. The Conservatives were on their last gasp of standing up to defend sort of traditional values.

We had months of discussions in the House of Lords about the well-being of children and in the end we had the interesting situation where two fairly right wing peers were challenged. We said to them. "You've stood up throughout all these debates and told us how dreadful the life-chances are for people who are brought up in care. So would you rather condemn children to being brought up in care rather than with a loving family, even if it's with just one parent, or with two parents of the same sex."

We'd got to the point where they simply had to say, "No! We do actually see the point you're making. Maybe it's is in the best interest of the children."

And that was the turning point – the key moment for all of the rest of the legislation that followed, both civil partnership and marriage – because it turned the whole argument around on its head.

You have two people who are trying to be responsible, trying to set up their personal situation in a way that encourages stability and responsibility, and yet you're trying to stop them from doing that. Why?

And they really didn't have an answer.

YOTAN OTTOLENGHI

I always knew I wanted children. It's probably in my genes,

because in Jewish culture not having a child is a big deal. But **t**here was a part of me felt that it wasn't right to have a completely gay family – two men with kids – I felt there needed to be a woman around, so we got into a couple of arrangements with women on co-parenting, but they didn't work out for various reasons.

The idea that you could have a complete gay family of two men with children took a while for me to get used to, but now, with two young boys, I feel it was completely unnecessary, almost ridiculous, to think we need to share the parenting with a woman in order to give the children a proper family.

REVEREND ANDREW FORESHEW-CAIN

My Bishop called me in when it was clear that I was going to get married and deployed every tactic he could think of – threatening me, cajoling me, persuading me – and finally actually ordering me not to get married. But I was determined not to be bullied out of it just because the bishop wanted me to wait until the church was ready.

I pointed out that I was 50, and that women had had to wait more than 40 years to be treated as almost equal to men (because in the *Church of England* they're still not treated as equal). I'd be dead by that time and I owed it to my husband not to deny him the marriage we both wanted.

CHAPTER
SIXTEEN

Last Word

YOTAN OTTOLENGHI

I think whether you're gay or straight matters less and less, and it's mostly a good thing. I see younger gay men these days, people that work with me, and for them it's becoming so much less of an issue.

YOTAN OTTOLENGHI

For me it really doesn't matter what the sexual orientation of my children is as long as they chose what's good for them.

STEPHANIE HIRST

Anybody can be attracted to anybody.

SIMON CALLOW

The big problem is if you're not having sex, that's when life gets difficult. Having sex is a delightful thing that can be accompanied by very intense feelings, but if you don't do it then it can all turn horribly wrong.

TOM ROBINSON

My bisexual side came round and smacked me round the back of the head and I found myself very inconveniently in love with a woman.

YOTAN OTTOLENGHI

That fluidity is something which makes so much sense.

EVAN DAVIS

I notice from young people that they just seem to mix everything up much more.

OLLY ALEXANDER

It's become more common; it's like an emerging kind of consciousness about these identities and sexual fluidity – gender fluidity.

STEPHANIE HIRST

I think the 50 years since the 1967 decriminalisation and

where we are today – look how far we have come.

LORD SMITH

You start with hatred and fear and then you move to tolerance, then you move to acceptance, but the real trick is to move from acceptance to celebration.

MATTHEW PARRIS

The fact is – fewer people give a toss about it.

STEPHEN FRY

There's a question you could ask gay people. You would have had to start asking them back in the Fifties and Sixties and Seventies, and come right up to today. Say there's a button in front of you and you can press it, and if you press it you won't be gay anymore – you absolutely won't be – you won't have any desire for anyone of your gender, you'll only have desire for people of the opposite sex and you'll be happily integrated into the heterosexual lifestyle. Would you press that button?

If during each decade a core group of gay people, say one hundred, had been asked this question, I think the results would be fascinating. I think you'd find it went from 95 buttons pressed back in the Fifties and Sixties, to virtually zero today. And that's incredibly important because...

It's not just about society accepting gay people, it's about gay people accepting themselves.

SIR IAN MCKELLEN (from his address to the Oxford Union, 2006)

We got rid of *Section 28*. We made it legal for gay people to serve in the military if they wanted to. We made it legal for gay people to teach. We made it illegal for anyone to be sacked on the grounds of sexuality. We established an equal age of consent, and now it is illegal to discriminate on grounds of sexuality. So how the world has changed. It used to be illegal to talk positively about homosexuality in schools and now it's required by the law, and that's been the revolution. But no, there's still more to be done...

Four or five years ago Michael was walking through Trafalgar Square. He'd just got a job as a civil servant as he'd been out of work and he and his husband or gay partner had their arms around each other celebrating. The pubs had just shut and as they passed the statues of the lions in the square three teenagers spotted the couple and shouted, "Queers, faggots, benders, shirt-lifters," all those charming expressions.

Michael was feeling pretty chipper and confident and he went up to them and said, "What's the matter? Yes, I'm gay...."

At which point a lad kicked him behind the knee and as his head hit the flagstone one of the girls who had high heels on stamped on his head. And she did it again. Until she killed him. In our capital city.

Now she's in prison of course. But where would she learn that? What did she think she was doing? What was it inside of her that made her think she could do that on the grounds that she didn't like the fact they were gay?

No one is born prejudiced. They learn it, and they can unlearn it very quickly. We're all members of these minorities. There's no such thing as the majority. It doesn't exist. Not a majority of sameness.

Thank God we're all different. As you look around here you see every single face is different. I mean it's wonderful isn't it? And if every face is different every personality is different. Every inside is different. And every sexuality could be different.

CONTRIBUTOR BIOGRAPHIES

Alexander, Olly

Harrogate-born Olly is a singer, songwriter and actor. He is the lead singer of the synth-pop band Years & Years. He has promoted safer sex and has been open about his struggles with depression, self-harm, eating disorders and anxiety from age 13 onwards.

Almond, Marc

Almond first began performing and recording in Soft Cell and has sold more than 30 million records as a solo artist. He spent a month in a coma after a near-fatal motorcycle accident in 2004. He has rejected being labelled a 'gay' artist because it allows people to marginalise his work.

Amos, Stephen K.

A stand-up comedian and television personality, he is a regular at the Edinburgh Festival Fringe and on the international comedy circuit. Amos is known for involving audience members during his shows. He studied criminal justice at the Polytechnic of Central London.

Barker, Baroness Liz

Liz Barker worked for Age Concern between 1983 and 2007 and was created a life peer in 1999. She is a Liberal Democrat spokesperson on the voluntary sector and social enterprise. She revealed she was in a same-sex relationship during the passage of the Marriage (Same Sex Couples) Act 2013.

Blame, Steve

Born near Chelmsford in 1959, he lived in Germany before becoming a UK-based news editor and presenter for MTV from 1987 and 1994. He hosted MTV's HIV/AIDS awareness campaign on World Aids Day and is now a screenwriter.

Browne, Lord John

Chief executive of the energy company BP between 1995 and 2007. Former President of the Royal Academy of Engineering and since 2001, a cross-bench member of the House of Lords. His book *The Glass Closet: Why Coming Out is Good Business* was published in 2014.

Callow, Simon

Actor, musician, writer and theatre director. Callow has written books on Oscar Wilde, Charles Laughton and Orson Welles. He came 28th in *The Independent*'s 2007 listing of the most influential gay men and women in the UK. He came out in 1984 in his book *Being An Actor*.

Cashman, Lord Michael

British Labour politician and former actor. His character in *EastEnders* took part in the first gay kiss in a British soap opera. He was a Member of the European Parliament from 1999 until 2014 and has been made a Labour peer in the House of Lords. He is a founding member of Stonewall.

Clary, Julian

Comedian, actor, presenter. Clary began appearing on television in the mid-Eighties and became known for his provocatively camp style. In 2012, he was the winner of *Celebrity Big Brother*. He has also acted in films and is writing novels for children.

Davis, Evan

An economist, journalist and presenter for the BBC. He was the BBC's economics editor before replacing Jeremy Paxman on *Newsnight*. He is also the presenter for BBC Two's venture-capital programme *Dragon's Den*, as well as Radio 4's *The Bottom Line*.

Eagle, Angela

A Labour politician who has been an MP since 1992. She has been a minister and shadow minister and, for a while, a challenger to Jeremy Corbyn for the party leadership, before standing down. She came out in a newspaper interview in September 1997.

Faye, Shon

Writer, presenter, editor, artist, Youtube vlogger and comedian, she is an activist for LGBTQ+ women's and mental health rights. She describes herself as "a modern career transsexual" who mostly writes "for attention". She also works helping Stonewall better engage with trans communities.

Foreshew-Cain, The Reverend Andrew

The first Anglican vicar to marry his gay partner in defiance of Church of England rules. He was a member of the General Synod and vicar of St Mary with All Souls, Kilburn, and St James in West Hampstead. He resigned as vicar claiming 'institutional homophobia' in the church.

Fry, Stephen

Comedian, actor, writer and presenter, he has acted on stage, film and TV as well being the reader for digital versions of the Harry Potter novels. He was one of the original cast of *Blackadder* and for 13 years was compere of the BBC quiz *QI*. He suffers from manic depression due to bipolar disorder.

Gambaccini, Paul

Born in the USA in 1949, he has lived in the UK since 1971. He is now one of Britain's best-known broadcasters, a radio and television presenter of programmes mostly about music or films. He has been a tireless activist on behalf of LGBT people and a profound critic of police tactics in hounding them.

Graf, Jake

A transgender actor, writer, and director, his first film was about his experiences in making a female-to-male transition, which he filmed throughout. Many of his stories emphasise the daily difficulties that trans men go through. In 2015 he was nominated for a Rainbow Award.

Hirst, Stephanie

A radio and TV presenter best known for hosting *Hit40UK*, the former national commercial chart show, and the weekday breakfast show on Capital Yorkshire. Stephanie announced she was in the process of gender transitioning during a live interview on BBC Radio5Live.

Hockney, David

World-acclaimed painter and major contributor to the Pop Art movement of the Sixties, he is considered one of the most influential artists of the 20th century. He lives in Yorkshire and California. One of his paintings sold for the highest price ever paid for a work by a living artist.

Jacobi, Sir Derek

His hugely successful stage career includes appearing in productions such as *Hamlet*, *Uncle Vanya* and *Oedipus the King*. He has twice won a Laurence Olivier Award and has starred in many films, such as *Day of the Jackal*, and in TV series as varied as *I, Claudius*, and *Last Tango in Halifax*.

John, Elton

Singer, pianist and composer, since 1967 Elton has sold more than 300 million records and collaborated with lyricist Bernie Taupin on more than 30 albums. His film scores include *The Lion King*; his stage credits, *Billy Elliot the Musical*; and in 1992 he established the Elton John AIDS Foundation.

Judd, Alain

In the Seventies he was the youngest member of the male chorus at Covent Garden Opera. Not only an operatic tenor and orchestral conductor, he is a respected interior designer with many rich and famous clients. He is also master of one of Britain's leading choirs, the Burgate Singers.

Lees, Paris

Journalist, presenter and transgender
rights activist, she topped
the *Independent on Sunday*'s 2013 *Pink List*
and came second in the 2014 *Rainbow
List*. She admits to having a soft spot
for good-looking Tories although she
profoundly disagrees with them.

Lucas, Matt

Comedian, screenwriter and actor, Lucas
met David Walliams at the National
Youth Theatre before working with
him on the TV show *Little Britain*. He is
a patron of the Karen Morris Memorial
Trust, a UK charity for leukaemia
patients. Though raised Jewish,
describes himself as a fairly secular Jew.

Lyons, Zoe

A stand-up comedian with a degree
in psychology, she has appeared
on *Mock the Week*, *Michael McIntyre's
Comedy Roadshow*, and *The Paul O'Grady
Show*. In 2004, Zoe won the Funny
Women Awards and is number 83 in
the *Independent*'s list of Britain's most
influential lesbians and gays.

McAdam, Mark

For 15 years a journalist and broadcaster for *Sky Sports*, specialising in football and interviewing Premiership players, he is the only gay sports reporter in Britain to have come out. *Attitude* magazine made him Bachelor of the Year in 2017.

McKellen, Sir Ian

His career spans Shakespeare to Harry Potter, from popular fantasy to science fiction, from Hamlet to Gandalf. He has received every major theatrical award in the UK and is showbiz's Number One champion of LGBT rights worldwide. In 2014 he was awarded Freedom of the City of London.

Ottolenghi, Yotam

An Israeli-British chef, restaurant owner and food writer. He is the co-owner of five delis and restaurants in London, as well as the author of several bestselling cookbooks. He is also a champion of LGBT rights. He met his partner in 2000 and married 12 years later. They have two sons.

Paddick, Lord Brian

Until his retirement in May 2007, he was the Deputy Assistant Commissioner in London's Metropolitan Police and Britain's most senior openly gay police officer. He was the Liberal Democrat candidate for the London mayoral elections of 2008 and 2012 and is now a Liberal peer.

Parris, Matthew

Political writer, broadcaster and author, he was formerly a Tory MP. Often controversial, he writes mainly for *The Times* and appears frequently on TV. In 1998, he outed Labour minister Peter Mandelson on *Newsnight* but claimed later he thought Mandelson had already done it himself.

Penna, Tris

Born in Cornwall, Penna is a former A&R man at EMI Records and MD of the record division of Andrew Lloyd Webber's Really Useful Group. He is now a successful record producer of albums of West End musical shows. He is also producer of a new musical about Dusty Springfield.

Prince, Jason

Singer, songwriter and DJ, he has
also produced records for artists as
diverse as Cilla Black, Rozalla, Gina
G, Angie Brown, Hazell Dean and the
Sleazesisters. He is a specialist HI-NRG
DJ on the Soho gay party scene and is
entertainment correspondent for the US
TV show *London Calling*.

Qboy

British rapper, songwriter, producer and
DJ, he was the first out gay rapper in
British hip-hop. He has performed as a
DJ and rapper at hip-hop events all over
the world. In 2007, he presented the
TV documentary *Coming Out to Class* for
Channel 4, about homophobic bullying
in schools.

Robinson, Tom

Radio presenter, LGBT rights activist and
rock star, he wrote *Glad to be Gay, 2-4-6-8
Motorway* and *War Baby*. He is married
and has two children but prefers not to
call himself bisexual, saying, "I'm a gay
man who happens to be in love with a
woman." He has a thrice-weekly show
on BBC Radio 6 Music.

Savage, Jon

Writer, broadcaster and music journalist, in 1991 he wrote a best-selling book on punk rock and the rise of the Sex Pistols, *England's Dreaming*. Since then he has written more books and contributed articles on music to many publications, including *Mojo* magazine and *The Observer*.

Sells, Dan Gillespie

The songwriter and vocalist for rock group The Feeling has two Stonewall awards – for Entertainer of the Year in 2007 and Entertainer of the Decade in 2015. He was co-parented by his father, his mother and his mother's partner Dilis, whom he calls "my other mum".

Sidhu, Manjinder Singh

Author, Youtube vlogger, counsellor and human rights activist, his book *Bollywood Gay* is a self-help manual for gay children of Indian immigrants, like himself. His vlogs include *Gay to Z Hindi*, *Sex Education & Sexual Problems in the Punjabi* and *How to Get Refugee Status if you're LGBT*.

Smith, Lord Chris

A former MP, cabinet minister and chairman of the Environment Agency, he was the first openly gay British MP, coming out in 1984. In 2005 he became the first MP to acknowledge that he was HIV positive. He is now Baron Smith of Finsbury, a Labour peer, and the master of Pembroke College, Cambridge.

Tatchell, Peter

Born in Melbourne, Australia, he came to London in 1971 and became a founder member of the Gay Liberation Front. Since then he has been Britain's foremost LGBT activist, forming OutRage! in the Nineties. It was rumoured he was offered a life peerage but had turned it down.

Todd, Matthew

Former editor of *Attitude* magazine between 2008 and 2016. His final issue featured Prince William on the cover – the first time a member of the royal family had posed for a gay magazine. He has written a play, *Blowing Whistles*, and his book, *Straight Jacket*, was shortlisted for the Polari Prize.

Tracey, Lee

For 40 years a top drag artist on the gay circuit, he has created hundreds of jokes for other entertainers and helped write Michael Barrymore's show in the Nineties. His autobiography *What Will the Neighbours Say!*, describes the horrific hospital treatments meted out to gay men in the Fifties.

Wardel, Mark

Wardel burst onto the London art scene in the Seventies with his modernist paintings of Boy George and other gay icons. In 2013, the V&A asked for 300 copies of the mask he created from a 1974 life cast of David Bowie, of which Bowie bought two copies for his own official archive.

Young, Will

Singer, songwriter and actor who won the first series of *Pop Idol* in 2002. He appears on TV, in films and on stage and was nominated in 2013 for the Laurence Olivier Award for Best Actor in a Musical. He gives talks in schools to help counter homophobic bullying.

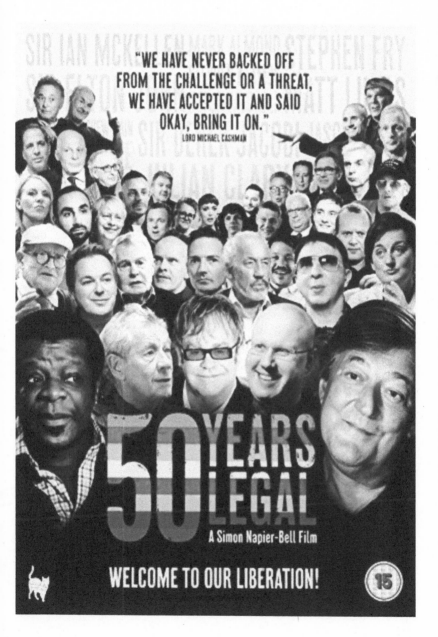

231

50 YEARS LEGAL
THE MOVIE
FULL TRANSCRIPT

PICTURE OF HEADLINES FROM VINTAGE NEWSPAPER CUTTINGS....
"How to spot a possible homo"
"What is a homosexual?"
"How sad when God's original design is twisted"

David Hockney: Well I'm an artist, I have to be honest; I mean I didn't want to deceive anybody really.
Paul Gambaccini: There was a profound sense of aloneness when you realised that you were different.

Archive footage of young gay men dancing in a café

Stephen Fry: The life one had to look forward to was one of secrecy, silence... I had no courage... I couldn't imagine coming out.
Matthew Parris: You found ways of being gay but you didn't talk about it.
Sir Derek Jacobi: I never made an announcement that I was gay. I always assumed that people knew.

TITLE: Production credits

David Hockney: The fact it was illegal, you didn't think about that much because you were just having sex with your friends.

Commentary on archive footage of young gays dancing: "The more he tries to deny her, the more womanish he becomes. Yes, woman is apparent in hermits, eunuchs, the chase and more than ever in them."

TITLE: *Production credits*

Simon Callow: For the most part the story was that it was an awful thing for people to be gay.
Paul Gambaccini: It didn't have a proper name.

TITLE: *Production credits*

Stephen Fry: André Gide is often considered the first person to use the word as a noun. 'You' are a homosexual, or 'I' am a homosexual.
Paul Gambaccini: Gay people were members of the Mattachine Society. And what now would be called lesbians were Daughters of Bilitis.

Commentary on archive footage of lesbians dancing: "One of the deep-rooted emotions that remove them completely from the company of man, yet at the same time cause them to emulate the masculine appearance with such pathetic results."

TITLE: *Production credits*

Simon Callow: I did know that I was attracted to other boys, or more importantly to men, from a very early age.
Will Young: I would say from like, four or five, I remember watching *Dynasty* and fancying Bobby more than fancying Krystle.

TITLE: *Production credits*

Sir John Wolfenden: Homosexual behaviour between adult consenting males in private should no longer be a criminal offence.

Stephen K. Amos: I think we all have to remember the people who have gone on before us where it was very much a political statement, where it was about people's lives that mattered.

TITLE: Production credits

Angela Eagle: There were just some very old-fashioned people in the Lords that seemed to be obsessed with what gay men particularly do in bed, and they compared it to bestiality and all sort of things.

Stephen K. Amos: Those people who didn't have a chance to blow a whistle or have rainbow flags or wear next to nothing marching up and down the street, but they were abused, spat at in the street. Those people who put their lives on the line to make it possible.

TITLE: Production credits

Paris Lees: I really try to practise gratitude, just for my mental health more than anything. I'm just so happy to be here and to be healthy because so many trans and LGBT people don't make it through.

Matt Lucas: My brother wasn't delighted when I told him I was gay. He went, "Oh great!" As if I'd just put in the coloured clothes with the white clothes.... "Oh great!"

FILM TITLE: 50 YEARS LEGAL

David Hockney: Sixty years ago I was painting homosexual propaganda. I knew everybody. Certainly there were a lot of gay people in Bohemia. I had a good time, actually, when I was young. I did.

Paul Gambaccini: I didn't even know that I was what would now be called gay because there was no frame of reference.

Stephen Fry: And it would be very different now because I would know straight away that I was gay because there'd be the whole internet laid out in apps and all kinds of things to ensure me that, not only I was gay but I fitted into precisely that category – I wasn't a bear or an otter or a twink, or all these extraordinary words that are used.

Matt Lucas: Homosexual is a brilliant word because there's something disdainful about it, it's sort of... It's handled with tweezers, isn't it! H-O-M-O-S-E-X-U-A-L.

Simon Callow: To be gay was clearly going to be just utterly depressing and doomed to loneliness and unhappiness, and you were going to be ostracised by your fellow human beings.

Angela Eagle: I just think it was bigotry, and it was also sheer horror and sometimes Biblical teaching.

Reverend Andrew Foreshew-Cain: Back in the Fifties the Church of England was a fundamental part of the start of the gay rights movement in this country. Since the Sixties, and since the support the archbishop gave to the Wolfenden Report and decriminalisation, it's been one of increasing sort of timidity and fear about sexuality.

Sir John Wolfenden: There are some actions, some forms of behaviour which most people would regard as sins, or at any rate as wrong, or as they say in some parts in England, not right.

Peter Tatchell: I think when the government appointed John Wolfenden they saw him as a safe pair of hands, their expectation was that he would recommend measures to control and constrain gay and bisexual men. The Wolfenden Report was a real breakthrough in that it recommended at least a partial decriminalisation of homosexuality, but John Wolfenden was not the saint that he's often portrayed as. He, in fact, was the main obstacle to a more progressive report.

Sir John Wolfenden: Now the problem for the legislators, as I see it, is to try to decide which of those actions that are regarded as morally wrong should be made into a crime.

Tom Robinson: When I fell in love with another boy at school I never told him. In that kind of level of loneliness and isolation and obsession I made a half-hearted suicide attempt. I woke up and found I was still alive and then it all came pouring out and that afternoon I was taken to a mental hospital in Cambridge. The thing about homosexuality, as I remember it, as it was presented to me – it was sin, it was a crime, and it was a disease, and in this instance they took the disease option and I was made to put my pyjamas on, get into bed, they took my temperature and they filled me full of drugs. What help is that to a desperate, lonely teenager at the end of his tether?

Lord Browne: That was one strand and the other strand was simply the illegality, and the great sensations in the press – that if you were gay you were bound to be a spy and that sort of thing.

Sir Derek Jacobi: The Burgess and Maclean case, that whole story was so, so extraordinary and magical. Burgess was such a personality. He was overtly homosexual and yet he got away with it.

Stephen Fry: There was a famous case involving Lord

Montagu of Beaulieu and a man called Peter Wildeblood. They were arrested for supposedly having nefarious sexual relations and they all pleaded not guilty, but Peter Wildeblood pleaded guilty and went to prison. He was probably one of the very first people ever to come out as gay.

Lord Cashman: The fact that there was this kind of combustible mix of peer-of-the-realm, a television executive, and men from the RAF exploded around Whitehall. And this directly led into the Wolfenden Report.

Sir Derek Jacobi: I was fascinated by it; I was also frightened as well as outraged. These people were demonstrating what I was and they were being persecuted for it.

Simon Callow: There were endless political scandals going on in the early Sixties and one of them concerned this rather insignificant naval attaché called William Vassall. I couldn't read enough about William Vassall because he was a gay man, and I wanted to know more about the lives of gay men.

Lord Browne: I went to university before the Wolfenden Report was enacted. I was the son of an Auschwitz survivor. All the context in which I lived was antithetical to being openly gay. My mother, you know, her lesson from Auschwitz was – never be an identifiable member of a minority.

Commentary on archive footage of men in a gay club: "It's estimated that one man in twenty is a homosexual. These men are a minority; they receive minority treatment; they face prejudice and intolerance and stand accused of depravity and vice."

Peter Tatchell: One of the first positive outcomes of the Wolfenden Report was the formation in the following year, 1958, of the Homosexual Law Reform Society. This was the first campaign group to work for law reform, to get the Wolfenden Report implemented.

Commentary on archive footage of men in a gay club: "Men who choose to love other men are treated not only with intolerance and contempt but prosecuted and jailed. As a result they become vulnerable to violence, blackmail and persecution."

Lee Tracey: I ended up trying to take my own life, cutting my wrists. I was found by a police car about half-past-four in the morning, frozen to death on the side of a road. They took me to the infirmary where I was sectioned and eventually they put me in a padded room and this guy, this nurse, put a tape recorder next to this bed and then he injected me and made me sick and vomit. While that's going on the tape recorder is playing, telling me what a filthy creature I am, and it's going on and on and on for three days and three nights. And I banged on the doors and screamed that I was cured, I was straight.

Lord Paddick: When I was born, homosexuality was illegal in the UK and, when on the rare occasion discussions about homosexuality came up at home, my parents made very clear what their views were and it was very hostile.

Marc Almond: I was never really aware that homosexuality was illegal until I saw a film called *Victim*.

Alain Judd: It was about a barrister who was married but he'd married outside of his inclinations.

Stephen Fry: My goodness the courage of Bogarde, who was a huge star for the Rank Organisation. There he was playing a barrister who was clearly gay, and indeed 'queer' is the word that's used, that is scrawled up on his garage door in the movie.

Commentary on archive film trailer of the film Victim: "What crime links him with this frightened boy on a building site? And why is he afraid?"

Alain Judd: He had this young man on the side and there were some nasty old queens in the pub and they blackmailed him.

Stephen Fry: And he has this wonderful speech: "I wanted him. I wanted him. Alright?"

Dirk Bogarde from the movie Victim: "I wanted him. Do you understand? Because I wanted him!"

Stephen Fry: It wasn't just, here's a sympathetic portrait of a gay person, it highlighted the wickedness of it all because the law was a charter for blackmail.

Lord Browne: I just decided very simply that I would create two lives, you know, a public life people saw and a private life that would be in so far as possible in the shadowy world of gay life. I would participate carefully.

Jon Savage: A lot of showbusiness and in particularly the music industry was run by old queens, or even middle-aged queens. The head of EMI, Sir Joseph Lockwood, was gay. The head of Decca, Ted Lewis, was gay. And the Beatles were managed by a gay man, Brian Epstein. He wasn't perhaps the fifth Beatle but they were certainly close to him and so they would have picked up on aspects of the gay experience.

Sir Derek Jacobi: The Beatles and everything, and yeah, I was typical I suppose at my age and my time. I did the gay clubs.

Commentary on archive footage of a Soho club: "Clubs that are merely one room with a bar at the top of a flight of Soho stairs."

Sir Derek Jacobi: There was one on the Kings Road.

Alain Judd: The Gigolo was... You went down the stairs because it was the basement in the shops above, and there was a little person behind a hole in the wall.

Sir Derek Jacobi: They were fun, and there was also the feeling that they were dangerous, which frightened me and yet attracted me.

Simon Callow: Once I went to work in the theatre I met lots of gay people, openly gay people, for the first time and clearly they weren't having a terrible time – they were having a great time, actually.

Sir Derek Jacobi: In the world of the arts the tolerance is amazing.

Lord Cashman: Performers were considered to be a bit affected and gay, that was kind of acceptable. But within the Establishment it was completely unacceptable because you had to learn to do it in private and not talk about it.

Woman speaking in archive footage: "But it was something I simply could not understand, that somebody could be gifted, talented, charming, lovable and at the same time a homosexual."

Commentary on archive footage of same woman: "This woman married a homosexual and twice during their marriage he was arrested for importuning. The second time he killed himself rather than face the punishment of a court."

TITLE: 1967 – Homosexuality Decriminalised

Mathew Parris: By far the biggest reform, by far the biggest step forward for gay people was the 1967 Act.

Peter Tatchell: The MPs and the Lords who backed law

reform in 1967 often did so begrudgingly and the undertone to their support was that gay people are poor pitiable creatures; we mustn't persecute them, they suffer this terrible affliction.

Lord Cashman: And it came about, I believe, not only because of the Wolfenden Report and the Wildeblood/Montagu case but actually from those women and men who went to prison, who lost their life, their liberty, because they would not conform.

Tom Robinson: Although legalisation had technically happened in '67, there were so many men going to prison for consensual sex over the age of 18 but under the age of 21. It was a nightmare.

Paul Gambaccini: The 'Pretty Police'. The youngest, best-looking police were tarted up and sent into public parks and public lavatories to entice gay men into making propositions, at which point they would be arrested. Thousands of people were arrested in this way.

Peter Tatchell: The Sexual Offences Act was not a legalisation of homosexuality; it was a very partial, limited decriminalisation.

Tom Robinson: There was an offence called gross indecency, which only applied to men, and it covered a whole range of conduct from a male-on-male kiss in a public place through to obviously cottaging, and what have you. And convictions for gross indecency actually rose by two hundred percent after 1967.

Peter Tatchell: So if I invited friends of mine down to London from Manchester to stay in my flat in my spare room, knowing that they were gay and could have sex, I was committing a criminal offence of aiding and abetting.

Lord Cashman: I knew I was gay. Luckily enough I was

an actor so I was amongst people where you could express yourself, but I couldn't hold a man's hand in the street or kiss or even chat a man up because that was soliciting, or importuning for immoral purposes.

Sir Derek Jacobi: Gross indecency, it was called. Gross indecency.

Commentary on archive material of men dancing in gay club: "A change in the law doesn't guarantee a change in attitude by the rest of us. For many of us this is revolting... men dancing with men."

Lord Smith: There was still profound inequality in place – the age of consent wasn't the same, there were all sorts of extra provisions about what you couldn't do, there was a battery of kinds and bits of statutes.

Marc Almond: You still felt you were part of that world of illegality; you still felt you had to kind of hide yourself to an extent.

Commentary on archive material of lesbians: "Lesbians. There is no law to stop them consenting privately to be lovers, and yet lesbians receive the minority treatment – intolerance, suspicion, often disgust."

Zoe Lyons: When I told my mum I was quite surprised that she was so surprised. I was never a girly girl. My room was adorned with pictures of Chrissie Hynde and Grace Jones, I had two Barbies and eight Action Men, and if I'm brutally honest the Barbies were just for the Action Men on their days off. What she said was... She sort of took it in and she said: "It's a little bit like being told your child's got cancer."

Angela Eagle: I think there's a lot of people internalising a lot of hatred. And 'shame' is a word that was used.

Will Young: Yeah, shame. Because shame is wrapped up with that sense of being different.

Olly Alexander: Shame lives within you for your entire life. It's a very complex and extremely powerful emotion, shame.

Zoe Lyons: I didn't want to be gay, I didn't want to be gay, I thought it would go away, and the advice was always – well it could always be just a phase, it's most likely a phase. And so I just kept thinking it will be a phase, and it will go away, and one day I will suddenly wake up and desire a husband and live in Surrey.

Angela Eagle: It's a very clichéd movie, *The Killing of Sister George*, because it's got such a caricature of the way gay women were. But anyway it was a pioneer of its time.

Actor 1 in footage of the movie The Killing of Sister George: "What a perfect little gem from the Sunday press, did it have to be here?"
Actor 2: "I'm sorry about the circumstances but I don't think it makes any real difference."
Actor 1: "No, of course you don't, because you planned it like this in the beginning."

Zoe Lyons: I thought the traditional view of a lesbian was that you were serious and slightly angry, and that... You know, because they were the only kind of people that were portrayed in films and in plays.

Angela Eagle: I don't recognise the lesbian life very much in it but, yes, it was obviously very important that it was even talked about.

Paul Gambaccini: I had come from a country where we were not allowed to exist.

Archive material of American man talking to crowd of school children: "There may be some here today that may be homosexual in the future, there are a lot of kids here, there may be some girls that will turn lesbian, we don't know, but it's serious. Don't kid yourself about it."

Peter Tatchell: In 1969 I read a small report about a gay rights protest in New York where reportedly hundreds or thousands of homosexuals had marched through New York demanding liberation. I'd read that report and I thought, "Yes! We've got to do that too."

Paul Gambaccini: People think that Stonewall might have been just a switching of a light and suddenly attitudes were different. Well consider how it was covered by the *New York Daily News*, which reported the headline: "Homo Nest Raided. Queen Bees Are Stinging Mad". And concluded, "The police are sure of one thing – they haven't heard the last from the girls of Christopher Street."

Lord Browne: I remember the movies like *Sunday Bloody Sunday*, and things like this.

Stephen Fry: Just the kiss, seeing the photograph of a kiss in a film, and to know there was film out there with that kiss in it. It was... It just sent shivers down the spine, it was extraordinary.

Actor in footage of the movie Sunday Bloody Sunday: "Are you alright?"

Lord Browne: To me it was an act of defiance. I actually wanted to join with that.

Peter Tatchell: When I arrived in London in August 1971, the Gay Liberation Front had not long been formed, and the Gay Liberation Front was really unique. For the first time, not hundreds but thousands of LGBT people came out, and we marched and protested. We demanded nothing less than our full emancipation. We had an agenda way beyond equality and law reform, we wanted to change society and change the culture. For us homosexuality wasn't the problem; it was society that was the problem.

Stephen K. Amos: When I think about growing up in London in the Seventies, a lot of people who, like me, had parents from either Africa or the Caribbean, we had one big deal – our issue was the race issue, because the one thing you cannot hide is your race, your ethnicity, you just can't hide it. But you can hide your sexuality, or your sexual orientation.

Stephen Fry: Oh, even a racist can't make a black man's skin white but in the past homophobia and sort of cultural homophobia has tried to make gay people straight, and that's a monstrous thing.

Peter Tatchell: The Gay Liberation Front had a definite strategy to challenge all the key homophobic institutions, from the church to psychiatry, the media, politics and so on.

Reverend Andrew Foreshew-Cain: That evangelical movement in the Sixties has grown in strength and contains within it an awful lot of people who are viscerally against gay and lesbian people.

Tom Robinson: Queer people were such a minority that people tended to club together. *Gay News* covered lesbian events as well as gay men's events and bisexual events.

Peter Tatchell: A very, very important stepping stone, because it was through *Gay News* that LGBT people across the country were connected and informed.

Tom Robinson: Buying *Gay News* from the newsstand was much more important than buying it from a seller in a gay pub, so it was walking up to somebody and saying openly, 'I want that newspaper'.

Simon Callow: I absolutely believe that the most important thing any gay person can do politically is just to come out.

Paul Gambaccini: I look back having lived through the entire history of activism, so the Mattachine Society became Gay Rights, Gay Pride, Lesbian and Gay Pride, LGBT etc. It evolves.

Peter Tatchell: The first Gay Pride march was in 1972. I can remember that less than a thousand people turned out.

Lord Smith: You start with hatred and fear and then you move to tolerance, then you move to acceptance, but the real trick is to move from acceptance to celebration.

Commentary on archive material of gays gathering in London to march: "Homosexuals have acquired a new pride and a new name, today they are called gays, and they are coming out on the streets of London."

Peter Tatchell: We were flanked virtually by a police officer for every single marcher, they hemmed us in, some of the officers openly shouted homophobic abuse and in those days there was nothing we could do.

Simon Callow: At first we were all very, very anxious, everybody was very anxious, police were anxious, they were out in force because who knew what would happen, but in fact... First of all people looked at us rather kind of curiously – What did homosexuals look like *en masse*? And then they seemed to think, well, they seemed to be having fun.

Paul Gambaccini: OK, we're going to march through central London, don't worry, wave, because if you wave at people they instinctively wave back. So we marched down Piccadilly and through the centre of London and we were all waving as if we were returning astronauts.

Paris Lees: I think a lot of LGBT people have this horrible shame that's been poured on them from when they were children.

Olly Alexander: You know, we have pride every year, which is super important, and I love being proud, but I guess 'proud' is the antithesis of 'shame'.

Paris Lees: That's why the pride movement is so important, it was about rejecting shame and saying, actually it's OK to be me and you're the one who's got the problem.

Tom Robinson: Come out, that was the total message of Gay Liberation, because you've got to live openly.

Matt Lucas: Gay used to be such a lovely word.

Tom Robinson: In those days 'gay' meant LGBTQI all the way down the alphabet.

Matt Lucas: I think representation of gay people in the media was such that gay people were either incredibly exotic and flamboyant like Quentin Crisp....

Quentin Crisp in archive material: "Well of course when I was young the world was very feminine."

Matt Lucas: Or Mr Humphries....

Mr. Humphries in archive material: "I would have been here at 8:58 but I caught my handbag in the lift."

Lord Cashman: Gay men in particular were only portrayed as either tragic and suicidal, or camp and mincing.

Jon Savage: When you look at Dusty Springfield... now she was one of the leading British female pop stars, if not the leading one, but certainly the best female artist and she seemed to be very emotionally vulnerable. Of course, that was because she was gay and she couldn't be honest about it.

Marc Almond: Growing up in the Seventies, I felt it was a thrilling exciting time but you didn't think of yourself as gay or homosexual or all the things like that. You didn't have those kind of labels put upon you then.

Stephen Fry: You just started to get the explosion of glam rock and what was variously called gender-bending and so on, and characters like Bowie, and then Elton John in '73 with 'Your Song', and so many of these glittery and sexually ambiguous figures began to point down the *Top Of The Pops* camera and beckon with their finger, and kids like me were going, 'Oh my gosh'! We could smell the danger.

Jon Savage: They were all unafraid to be camp.

Marc Almond: You could hide behind glam rock, you could wear makeup for the first time, you could express yourself with coloured hair or clothes that you wore, and nobody thought necessarily you could be gay, you could just be into glam rock.

Peter Tatchell: David Bowie's coming out was a pivotal moment.

Archive material of David Bowie singing

Tom Robinson: Bowie sang "you're not alone" and we weren't.

Steve Blame: Well I was 13 when Bowie announced that he was gay and for me this was obviously an impactful thing that happened because I was a teenager and I was starting to also have feelings for the same sex.

Stephen Fry: I was astonished by the idea that somebody could say to a journalist they were homosexual. And then everyone is going, "No, he's bisexual." And all these very straight fans of Bowie who had gone into school colouring their hair and cutting it like Aladdin Sane.

Jon Savage: Bowie was absolutely central, the interview with *Melody Maker* with Mick Watts in January 1972 was the key moment. It was five years after homosexuality had been partially decriminalised and he said, "I'm gay." Hello, you know, a door opens.

Marc Almond: And then you had punk and you had post-punk and New Romantics and all these things – disco, all these things you went through in the Seventies really enabled you to have disguises.

Stephen Fry: Yes, there were political figures and there were marches and gay liberation and people who wore the T-shirts and pumped the fists and all the rest of it and they are important, but always, it is artists and people, the cutting edge of popular culture and high art, who make the most difference.

Lord Cashman: Music and popular culture drove the political agenda.

Peter Tatchell: *The Naked Civil Servant* was an incredibly moving, powerful film and I think for people who identify as trans it was also particularly significant.

Stephen Fry: His courage and his strength, and that's what John Hurt managed to convey, as well as much as anything; the way he could walk with his head held high.

Tris Penna: Well, I thought it was empowering seeing John Hurt walking down the street. I think at that point I would have dyed my hair orange, it was like, "Fuck off everybody."

Quentin Crisp in footage of The Naked Civil Servant: "I am an effeminate homosexual, I want to win the admiration, I want to be found desirable by a great dark man."

Stephen Fry: What was interesting to me about that was that I didn't even think it was really about a gay man. I thought it was about a unique individual, because Quentin Crisp and I shared absolutely nothing in common in terms of our style, he was a piece of performance art.

TITLE: 1977 – 10 Years Legal

Peter Tatchell: Tom Robinson's Seventies hit song 'Glad to be Gay' was the queer national anthem.

Archive footage of Tom Robinson singing the verse of 'Glad to be Gay'

Matthew Parris: 'Sing If You're Glad to be Gay' meant a huge amount to me and I actually went to Fairfield Halls in Croydon to watch him and felt very brave.
Peter Tatchell: It was such a positive affirmation of our right to be and such a damning indictment of the homophobia we faced.

Archive footage of Tom Robinson singing the chorus of 'Glad to be Gay'

Tom Robinson: It was clear that something was going to erupt and that you had to nail your colours to the mast and say, "So try and sing you're glad to be gay with all that." And it was a furious song.
Marc Almond: The beginning of the Eighties, when I first had success and the public became aware of me, was the most frightening time of my life. Before then it had all been kind of good times, a little bit clandestine, and you got to the club and you would knock on the door.
Will Young: Gay clubs in the Eighties, it's got a heat to it, it has a sort of smell to it.

Stephen Fry: And it seemed to be a wild party that would never end.

Steve Blame: What do you go to a nightclub for? You went to a nightclub to drink, to listen to music, to take drugs and to have sex, to have a great time. And I had no reservations.

Matt Lucas: The thing is people say, "Oh gay people are promiscuous." But I don't think it's gay people who are promiscuous; it's men. Men like to have sex. I think if straight men had sex with each other they would be just as promiscuous. It's about men, because men are dogs.

Marc Almond: I had a lot of big hits at the beginning of the Eighties which, when you look back at those TV appearances now, with a leather mirror cap, with eyeliner, they are shockingly outrageous really for *Top Of The Pops* at that time.

Archive footage of Marc Almond singing with Soft Cell

Jon Savage: Soft Cell are very important, they were huge, they were very obviously deviant – the video for 'Tainted Love'..., and then they did a video for a song called 'Sex Dwarf'. They were hilarious, and they were brilliant, and they were touching, and they were emotional.

Stephanie Hirst: During the Eighties people like Marc Almond being able to express themselves the way they were, Boy George, the Blitz, all that kind of thing, was because people could be their true selves.

Mark Wardel: Blitz was incredible. It was full of very ambitious, mostly gay people.

Young man interviewed in archive material: "Blitz is about people who... Young people who want to be different and want to be surrounded by other people who are also different."

Mark Wardel: People who were at the Blitz, who were gay people, like Boy George and Steve Strange, what they were doing was they were inventing an exaggerated persona.

Interviewer to Boy George in archive material: "Have you always looked like this?"
Boy George in archive material: "Well, I don't think I have an image anyway, I mean I just dress up, I'm an eccentric and that's that."

Will Young: Very clever because it's sort of utter expression but also his real ambition at the same time.
Mark Wardel: The first time I saw Boy George he had two-foot high hair with stuffed parrots in it and a kimono, and the makeup was just beyond.
Will Young: Boy George was like a lifeline really, it was someone who was public, and gay, and themselves.

Archive footage of Boy George singing 'Do You Really Want to Hurt Me'

Steve Blame: Boy George was putting up a front to appear to be the non-sexual, acceptable homosexual of that time. Boy George always used to say that he preferred a cup of tea to sex.
Julian Clary: It was very competitive, you had to do something unusual, it was the Eighties. I wasn't the only one wearing makeup and I'm very softly spoken, so I thought if I wear a lot of makeup, and take a dog on stage with me this might give me some momentary advantage.
Evan Davis: You were in the world of 'don't ask don't tell' and actually there was a very big moment. I can remember this moment, I was in the car and Andy Bell of Erasure

was being interviewed on the radio and he referred to his boyfriend and there was no deep intake of breath. That was the goal, that you could just talk about it like that without it being a big deal.

Interviewer to Marc Almond in archive material: "Why do you think it is that so many people gossip about you?"
Marc Almond in archive material): "Because there is plenty to gossip about."

Marc Almond: When I finally said... When a journalist came to my house badgering me as they always did in interviews, so I said, "Fuck it! Yeah, I'm gay, I'm a faggot, I'm gay gay gay gay gay gay gay gay." After that there was no going back. I desperately did try to climb back into the closet a little bit but the door was locked by that time and it was too late. And I hated that journalist with a vengeance because I thought, "He made me do that."

Jon Savage: Out of that gender-bending moment came Bronski Beat's 'Smalltown Boy'. Jimmy Somerville didn't act gay, he wasn't dressing up.

Marc Almond: He presented himself in a checked shirt and jeans and a crew cut. In other words, "I'm a gay person and I look just regular."

Jon Savage: He looked like a straight man. And of course that is every straight man's biggest fear.

Mark Wardel: People at the time who were really political and outspoken about it – people like Holly Johnson.

Archive material of Frankie Goes to Hollywood singing 'Relax'
Archive news broadcast. Newscaster 1: The lifestyle of some male homosexuals has triggered an epidemic of a rare form of cancer.

Archive news broadcast. Newscaster 2: They have found several cases where people who had been sex partners both have the condition.

Archive news broadcast. Newscaster 3: Up to 17,000 people in England and Wales...

Archive news broadcast. Newscaster 4: ....will die of AIDS in the next four years. Laboratory tests show between 20,000 and 50,000 in England and Wales have been infected with the HIV virus.

Simon Callow: Something was happening, the 'summers of love' had turned into something a little bit more driven and obsessive. People now began to think that having sex was a duty – you had to have it... if you hadn't had sex on any one day you had failed in life, and preferably sex two or three or four times with two or three, or four different people.

Stephen Fry: Its timing was extraordinary. It seemed you could almost believe some of the wild preachers in America who claimed it was 'God's punishment', because it came at the very crest of the reaping of the rewards of the early Gay Liberation movement.

Reverend Andrew Foreshew-Cain: When I was at university the local church had a post board out of it saying, "AIDS, the wrath of God."

Simon Callow: There was a frenzy going on and somehow it erupted into AIDS. I'm not saying even that it was caused by it, by any means, but it was a phenomenon that sprang up in our midst with the most terrifying intensity.

Paul Gambaccini: Of course America preceded Britain. The gay capitals of America preceded Britain, and when I returned to a still sleeping London, I said to my housemates, "From now on fucking is banned in this house."

Peter Tatchell: 1981 was the beginning of the AIDS

pandemic and the AIDS panic.

Stephen Fry: One saw, because it was like a war, you saw as you do in wars both the best and worst of what humans can be. You can see glorious heroism and you can see terrible cowardliness and cruelty.

Peter Tatchell: Initially gay people, through organisations like the Terrence Higgins Trust, were the only responders, and that's partly because it hit our community first. We faced massive government indifference. For the first few years the government of Margaret Thatcher sat on its hands and did nothing.

Stephen Fry: HIV arrived in the Western world and ploughed its deadly furrow through the societies of America and Britain and Europe and elsewhere, primarily Africa, of course. During that time a lot of my friends had to tell their parents they were gay and in the same sentence tell them they were going to die very soon, and die one of the most horrible deaths.

Elton John: During the years when AIDS started to happen and during the Eighties and the beginning of the Nineties I wasn't there. I got sober in 1990 and I looked back on my life and I thought I didn't do enough. I wasn't really at the heart of the anger which I should have been at, and I lost so many friends I couldn't figure out why I had been so absent from this fight against AIDS.

Tris Penna: It wasn't until the mid-Eighties that you knew anything really about it. It was just a lot of people in America – lots of people in America dying, and people older than me dying. And then suddenly it was people that I knew, younger people dying.

Peter Tatchell: Whilst gay men were dying they were just not interested, but as soon as the first heterosexual men contracted AIDS then suddenly the government leapt into action.

Archive news broadcast: The health minister warns heterosexuals and appeals to everyone to avoid casual sex.

Paul Gambaccini: And there were a lot of people in authority saying, "Good, you're dying."

Julian Clary: There were things going on that you couldn't make up, really. James Anderton, the chief of police in Manchester...

Archive news broadcast: Mr Anderton told a conference that people at risk were swirling around in a human cesspit of their own making.

Julian Clary: ...saying that gay people were the spawn of Beelzebub. And there were police raids on the Vauxhall Tavern with all these policemen wearing rubber gloves, things like that, which is like a comedy sketch really. It's outrageous and insulting but it is quite funny.

Paul Gambaccini: And everybody used the word 'gay plague'.

Simon Callow: The ghastly parade went on and on and on and on. It went on for years. The funerals, the funerals. Oh, unbearable. Visits to hospitals. The helplessness.

Paul Gambaccini: We were used to fighting, we had the necessity to be activists.

Steve Blame: I used to go to a club called Lazers, which was in North London, once a week and this was in something like 1982. Ten years later when I was working for MTV I did an interview in that club and the Greek owner was in the club that day and I asked him, "Why did you shut the club?" And he said to me, "Everyone died."

Stephen Fry: I would find myself sitting on the bed of a boy with whom I had been at university with. He was a dear friend who was looking skeletal and dreadful, waxy skin and Kaposi sarcoma on the legs, and their parents would sit with them, tear-filled eyes, and next to them is the boy's lover, partner, who for some reason is not HIV positive and they're thinking, "You did that to my boy."

Mathew Parris: If assisted dying had been allowed in those days there would be quite a few people who would have simply taken their own lives. I was as prey as everybody was to the sudden terror that I had contracted the virus. I worked out how I was going to take my own life.

Lord Smith: The government was responding a little bit alarmed but, nevertheless, quite well in terms of resources they were putting in to the advent of HIV and AIDS.

Government minister in archive news broadcast: "This is a mock-up of the front cover, and as I say, that will be going out to every household in the country."

Paul Gambaccini: We had the health information campaign, which peaked famously with the John Hurt Iceberg.

John Hurt Iceberg commercial: "The virus can be passed during sexual intercourse with an infected person, anyone can get it, man or woman. So far it's been confined to small groups, but it's spreading."

Tris Penna: It always struck me as being so unfair. You know, when I was born it was illegal to be gay... partly decriminalised, and then in the Seventies to be hated, and in the Eighties that had to land on your doorstep.

Simon Callow: And in the face of all that, how the fuck could you care about whether people knew you were gay or not?

Lord Smith: Gradually, and this happened very gradually, people in all walks of life, people in your neighbourhood, in your workplace, in your family, began to be open about who and what they were.

Lord Cashman: Chris Smith, on a public platform, came out, and it took our breath away.

Lord Smith: It was only when I walked into the hall and I suddenly thought – actually, now's the time to say something. It was my turn to speak; I stood up; I said, "My name is Chris Smith. I'm the Labour MP for South Finsbury, and I'm gay." And at that point the entire hall got to its feet and gave me a standing ovation.

Stephen Fry: I think AIDS was an accelerant towards acceptance of couples, and it was an accelerant towards the acceptance of gay people, that in a sense, whether they were conscious of it or not, ordinary straight people understood that they had gone through something.

Archive news broadcast: "The miners in Lancashire are to be instructed to join the strike."
Archive news broadcast: "Police move forward en masse in a manoeuvre well tried and tested."
Miner's activist in news archive broadcast: "It's only over the last year that we have come to know gay and lesbian people."

Angela Eagle: When the Labour movement itself actually realised that those who were oppressed needed to fight together, a solidarity of lesbians and gay people supported the miners with the miner's strike.

Paul Gambaccini: And at the front of the queue were the trannies, meaning Lily Savage, Regina Fall, people like this.

Lee Tracey: The problem with the miners, you can't not support people that are starving to death, you know... they were starving to death, they literally were starving.

Tom Robinson: You either live in a free and fair, equal society or you don't. You can't fight for just that one little group.

Stephen Fry: The important thing is, I think, it's the connection gay people make when they see what is happening in their own relatively small community... it's very hard not to connect it to the wider world of disadvantaged, marginalised people.

Elton John speaking in Washington in archive footage: "Because of their HIV positive status, because of their sexuality, because of their poverty, they feel marginalised and left out. We have to replace the shame with love; we have to replace the stigma with compassion. No one should be left behind."

TITLE: 1987 – 20 Years Legal

Margaret Thatcher in archive news broadcast: "Children who need to be taught to respect traditional moral values are being taught that they have an inalienable right to be gay. All of those children are being cheated of a sound start in life. Yes, cheated."

Angela Eagle: I came into parliament living through Thatcherism. There was a real change of mood in the country that wasn't being reflected in our politics.

Lord Cashman: A lot of our information that wasn't

scurrilous came from the gay bisexual media, like *Capital Gay*.

Lord Smith: When the offices of *Capital Gay* newspaper in London had been firebombed, one of the Labour London MPs was on his feet in the House of Commons, and was condemning the firebombing, and Elaine Kellett-Bowman shouted out, "It was quite right." It wasn't a happy atmosphere. It was the time of *Section 28* coming in.

Lord Cashman: Into that mix, the BBC introduced the first same-sex kiss in a soap, *EastEnders*.

Matt Lucas: There was no one who was gay who didn't appear to me to be basically an alien. The normalisation of it didn't happen probably until, for me, seeing Michael Cashman on *EastEnders*.

Lord Cashman: Colin, that I played, and Barry – these two gay characters, ordinary men, they ordinarised homosexuality.

Matt Lucas: It was a radical, progressive brave thing for the BBC to do.

Lord Cashman: The front page of *The Sun* was "East Benders". When I went into the show they outed my partner to his family in the *News Of The World* with the centre pages, "Secret Gay Love of AIDS Scare EastEnder." And that afternoon a brick came through the window. Do you back off because that happened? Strangely enough, it makes you stronger.

Archive news broadcast: "Four lesbian demonstrators broke into the studio of the BBC's Six O'Clock News as it was going on air tonight and began shouting protests."
Archive news broadcast: "The women were protesting that the Lords had approved a clause banning local councils from promoting homosexuality."

Paul Gambaccini in archive footage from TV show: "I was completely devastated. Never before have I lived in a country which has voluntarily taken backwards steps in the areas of personal liberty."

Lord Smith: There had been a big row about a book called *Jenny Lives with Eric and Martin*. The press had gone bananas over this book, on how dreadful it was that perversion was being taught to children.

Dan Gillespie-Sells: I was raised from the age of about one by two women and I'm super proud of them because they did it at a time that was not so easy, during *Section 28*. It talked about not legitimising this alternative idea of a family.

Olly Alexander: At school, I mean I just had no awareness of any gay people really, any queer people.

QBoy: You're not at that age really ready to deal with your sexuality, to acknowledge it, you're not even thinking about it most of the time. So for other people to then tell you, "Oh, you're gay." And persecute you for it as well, like it's a bad thing. It's quite difficult. 'Queer boy' is what they used to call me at school.

Olly Alexander: I mean, I knew I was gay but I was still telling myself I could be straight.

Jake Graf: My mother and father were very loving and very caring but obviously had no information or no resources. And again, transgender back then wasn't discussed at all.

Matt Lucas: I regard Margaret Thatcher and the people who created and endorsed *Section 28* as murderers because they prevented young men from learning how not to contract AIDS and die.

Archive material of a spokesman for the Terence Higgins Trust: "How

do you promote safer sex for gay men without being charged with
promoting homosexuality?"

Paul Gambaccini: Well, you can't talk about men having
sex because that's promoting men having sex. It was like
Douglas Hurd, who was the Home Secretary, saying that you
couldn't use condoms in prison, mainly because they couldn't
admit that men were having sex with each other in British
prisons.

Government minister in archive news broadcast: "Now let's take
condoms, if you were to introduce condoms into prisons – I think
you would have the effect of encouraging people to do what they
wouldn't otherwise do."

QBoy: I remember distinctly at age nine, it was the first time
that I was called gay. My form tutor, I would say to her, this is
happening and she would actually say, 'I'm not able to help
you with this.'

Stephen K. Amos: And to any young child going through
the turmoil of finding out who they are and not having access
to information, wow, that's so damaging.

QBoy: My head of year went out of his way, because he was
gay, to try to help me and he got into trouble once with the
head teacher.

Shon Faye: The very fact is that when you were being
homophobically   bullied, teachers were not allowed...
teachers were too afraid to say anything to comfort LGBT
pupils. They were too afraid to tell you even in private that it
was OK to be gay.

Will Young: It's a society where being gay is very much
seen as wrong and not the norm and, if anything, when

you're young people want to fit in, because it's the ones that don't fit in that are bullied.

Shon Faye: It creates a culture of silence in which prejudices start themselves to go unquestioned. People should be on guard for homophobic bullying in schools because often you're so ashamed about it and you don't want to say, because you think telling someone that you have been homophobically bullied means telling someone you're gay, and you're not willing to do that.

Manjinder Singh Sidhu: So I used to try to imagine my life with a woman... so I used to say I can change this thought, because I wasn't taught this at school and *Section 28* was in existence then and they couldn't talk about homosexuality. So I used to try and brainwash myself every night, for a good half an hour, to make myself straight.

Angela Eagle: It's an absolutely appalling piece of legislation which is a stain on our country.

Matt Lucas: You have to remember there was a moment when there wasn't *Section 28* and then it came in. It wasn't something that they inherited. It was something that they initiated. Fuck 'em!

Sir Ian McKellen onstage in archive news material: "I'm here because I'm one of millions of normal homosexuals who are affected by this new law. *Section 28* is in parts designed to keep us in our place, but it didn't work with me."

Paul Gambaccini: Coincident with, or perhaps as a result of, Ian McKellen's courageous denunciation of *Section 28*, Stonewall was set up as a charity.

Lord Cashman: And our aim was to ensure another *Section 28* never happened again.

Paul Gambaccini: Ian said to me, when we were founding the charity for gay rights to fight *Section 28*, "But we need money."

Lord Cashman: As luck would have it I bumped into Billy Connelly and complained that his manager, John Reed, never returned my calls. And Billy said to me, "It's nothing personal, he doesn't return my calls either." So that afternoon John rang me and he said, "OK, come over for dinner."

Paul Gambaccini: So Ian, Michael Cashman and myself went over for dinner at John Reed's house, and Elton was there, and at the end of dinner, John said, "So what is it that you hope to achieve?" And Michael gave a very elegant summary of the goals of Stonewall.

Lord Cashman: And Elton suddenly went, "John, so Michael has been telling me about Stonewall." And he said, "I'm giving them fifty thousand." And a long pause, and John went, "I'll match it."

Paul Gambaccini: And that was it, that was the founding of Stonewall, the financing of Stonewall was achieved in one dinner.

Peter Tatchell: Stonewall was essentially the suffragists, the ones who lobbied governments and things through the respectable traditional routes. OutRage! was more the suffragettes. We took direct action; we confronted homophobes and institutions face to face. We were doing direct action to force the LGBT issue on the agenda.

Lee Tracey: Political activists actually turned... they made other people feel uncomfortable. If you've got a singer or a comedian or a dancer on a stage or a television show, they have got fans from all sorts of people, straight people, gay people, and that's what breaks down the barriers.

Simon Callow: My belief is that there is an essential underlying acceptance of homosexuality; it's something to do with our tradition of camp and all of that, and our odd cross-dressing and traditions in the theatre.

Zoe Lyons: Well, the thing with comedy is that there is a very, very strong connection with gay humour in British comedy.

Julian Clary: All the things that were going to be a problem, I was told, in my life – my mannerisms and my voice – things that might have got in the way of other careers, somehow in comedy, certainly when I started doing it, these could be used to your advantage.

Excerpt of Julian Clary in archive comedy footage: "Right! What sticky substance do you find down Daley Thompson's jock strap? Stick your hand up if you know."

Julian Clary: Talking graphically about gay sex, it all seemed to fit into that, without really thinking about it or planning it.

Matt Lucas: For me, my whole thing was to try and lay as many clues as possible. So for instance, as a teenager I was an actor, and then I started doing stand-up comedy, but I did it in character and I played this character as this gay old actor, rather like 'The Only Gay in the Village'.

Excerpt of Matt Lucas in archive comedy footage: "Bloody hell I'm so down."
Actor: "Oh, why is that David?"
Matt Lucas: "Don't you know I'm the only gay in this village. Oh I just dream of the day I could just meet other gays who know what it's like to be a gay."

Zoe Lyons: I guess I'm lucky in that I have never had any brutal horrific homophobia thrown at me. I have had the occasional, "Dyke!" from a white man.

Zoe Lyons in live performance (archive material): "I think homophobia would be a lot more acceptable if it was a little bit more like arachnophobia, rather than the awful crime it really is. It would genuinely mean you were terrified of finding a gay in your bathtub."

Zoe Lyons: Somebody shouted out lesbian on stage and the whole audience turned on the bloke and it was great, just wonderful.

Stephen K. Amos in live performance (archive material): "Who here tonight is an out and proud gay man?" AUDIENCE RESPONSE Sings: "I'm coming out."
"Who's an out and proud lesbian?" AUDIENCE RESPONSE
"Well done. Who's an out and proud bisexual?" AUDIENCE RESPONSE
"There is always a couple.... I'll take anything."

Stephen K. Amos: I've just done this thing, a very silly joke, recently where I'm talking about social media and I say that before social media I had my own inner circle of like-minded friends with the same ideals and same beliefs, that was my inner circle of friends. But now because of social media my circle has been widened by dicks. That's clearly a non-gag; that's just a joke.

Lee Tracey: When you can laugh at yourself you can laugh with other people... At you.

Jason Prince: The Nineties started off as what we would say is 'gay club fever'. People like Rozalla with 'Everybody's Free' was a gay club anthem, and then before we knew it, it was a straight club anthem.

Archive footage of Rozalla singing 'Everybody's Free'

Reverend Andrew Foreshew-Cain: In the early Nineties, before I had met Stephen, I used to go clubbing rather a lot, so a lot of house, where in the Nineties when I was dancing with my T-shirt off, when I could dance with my T-shirt off, in clubs all across London. I was a curate in South London and we used to go to the Fridge and Heaven.

Jason Prince: The gay club scene 20 years ago was really a refuge for gay people to feel safe in among their own kind. At the time, obviously, there was a lot of prejudice, it was still very difficult, especially for young gay people to come out.

Will Young: Nightlife and community in music for gay people is... represents family, lifeline, safety, friendship, relationships, sex.

Matthew Todd: I think we went through a huge commercialisation of culture generally, so mainstream culture and gay culture too in the Nineties. I think for a long time people felt that was a really positive thing, because the whole concept of pink power meant that gay bars sprang up everywhere.

Paris Lees: You would have been more likely to have met an alien than a trans person in the mining town where I come from. Just growing up and realising that I am trans and thinking, 'oh my God, I'm one of those people that are just ridiculed'.

Archive material of football crowd chanting

Peter Tatchell: When Justin Fashanu came out in 1990 it was a real breakthrough. He was the first and only Premier League player to ever come out.

Mark McAdam: I don't think anyone really understands the pressure that is on these players, the pressures that Premier

League players would face having to come out.

Stephen K. Amos: To have this burden on his shoulders when he was hiding something else much to the disapproval of his family... He was disowned by his own brother, the fellow footballer John Fashanu, and denounced in *The Voice* newspaper as bringing shame to the black community. He was battling against a manager at Nottingham Forest, Brian Clough, who was overtly homophobic and abused him in a homophobic manner.

Mark McAdam: Football is such a masculine environment. It's dominated by image, perception and in the way you have to act.

Peter Tatchell: Conflict over his faith and sexuality, the demise of his football career. It weighed so heavily on him, you could see him going down, down, down and down.

Mark McAdam: That's what makes the Justin Fashanu thing even sadder. He got put in a situation where he had to take his own life.

Peter Tatchell: It was a tragedy.

Archive news broadcast: "If you're 16, male and homosexual you can face two years behind bars because the age of consent for that category is still 21."

A man being interviewed in archive news broadcast: "I don't believe that these youngsters should be encouraged by this government of all – back to basics and family values – in reducing the age from 21 to 18, 16, or whatever."

Sir Ian McKellen in archive news broadcast: "I think the Home Secretary will really have to announce to the house today what his proposition would be for the treatment of 16 and 17-year-old gay men who were having sex with each other."

Jason Prince: I met my first long-term boyfriend when I was 17. My relationship with David was illegal for the first four or five years because at the time, of course, the age of consent was 21.

QBoy: At that time I had already started having sexual relations with other boys from quite an early age. So I was aware that I was breaking the law.

Male MP in archive news clip of House of Commons debate: "What my honourable friend is trying to do is to get this house to vote to legalise the buggery of adolescent males."

Edwina Currie in archive news clip: "For a long time I was very puzzled – why did some of my male colleagues feel so frightened of gay men?"

Stephen Fry: Why is someone making such a fuss? It can only be because there was some part of themselves that is unhappy, uncomfortable, frightened – and that's very revealing.

Mathew Parris: John Major, who first lowered the age of consent. Or rather John Major gave parliament the opportunity to do it, knowing they would do it, and it was lowered from 21 to 18.

Archive news broadcast: The Bishop of Bath and Wales believes the law should provide a breathing space until they're certain of their sexuality.

Stephen Fry: In a sense it's more recent that the church has become, or various churches and religious have become, the more obvious public enemies of acceptance of homosexuality, but it was a purely social cultural thing before that, the churches didn't really have much to say about it.

Peter Tatchell: In the Nineties, the then Archbishop of Canterbury, Dr George Carey, refused to meet or dialogue with any LGBT community organisation.

Reverend Andrew Foreshew-Cain: The conservative evangelicals in the Church of England would say that the Bible says being gay is wrong – homosexual genital acts, as they like to refer to them, are condemned in scripture, and it's not possible to be a practising homosexual and a Christian.

Sir Ian McKellen speaking in a music video clip: "Homosexuality is only a polite deceptive euphemism for the most bestial obscenity (in capital letters) and a degrading, disgusting unnatural sexual perversion contrary to the divine law of the almighty God."

Reverend Andrew Foreshew-Cain: And they take a very strict Biblical line based on seven verses in the whole of Christian scripture.

Peter Tatchell: OutRage! tried to have a dialogue, we were rebuffed. We went to Canterbury Cathedral on Easter Sunday to challenge the Archbishop on his defence.

News clip of Peter Tatchell: "Doctor Carey supports discrimination against lesbian and gay people; he opposes lesbian and gay human rights; this is not a Christian teaching."

Peter Tatchell: Seven of us walked into the pulpit holding up placards criticising Doctor Carey's support for legal discrimination against LGBT people.

News clip of Peter Tatchell: "Up until the time we staged our protest at Canterbury Cathedral the Archbishop of Canterbury had refused to meet with lesbian and gay organisations. Since our protest he has finally met for the first time with the Lesbian and Gay Christian Movement."

TITLE: 1997 – 30 Years Legal

Archive news broadcast: A nail bomb went off tonight in a crowded pub in central London.
Archive news broadcast: "The device exploded around 6:30. People there have spoken of individuals being thrown 30 feet across the road by the force of the blast. The focal point of London's gay community, a bomb ripped apart the Admiral Duncan pub. It was an event that was to take homophobic violence to a new and unprecedented level."

Stephen K. Amos: In that week there was a bomb in Brixton market and then there was a bomb somewhere in the East End, so it was very much a scare campaign for any minority. And then someone like me, black and gay, thinking, "Oh my God, they've attacked my community twice."

Lord Cashman: We thought we were through the worst of what had happened to our community, and then for this to happen was almost unimaginable, and I think unbearable.

Stephen K. Amos: That kind of atrocity brought different communities together, it showed that there are people out there who see us all as deviants and wrong, and as I was saying, that we should all be annihilated.

Lord Cashman: LGBT communities have been brilliant. We've never backed off from the challenge, the threat. We've accepted it and said, OK, bring it on.

Archive footage of military band marching and playing at Gay Pride

Peter Tatchell: Two major gay law reforms in Britain were the end to the ban on lesbian and gay people serving in the armed forces, and the equalisation of the age of consent.

MP in archive footage of televised debate in House of Commons: "To maintain an unequal age of consent sends out a message of discrimination."

Peter Tatchell: But both of those were not brought in initially by the Labour government. They were the result of adverse rulings in the European Court of Human Rights.

Lord Smith: The Prime Minister, Tony Blair, was really nervous about doing any of it; he was worried about what the public impact was going to be, what the press will think.

Angela Eagle: Bit by bit, brick by brick, we knocked that wall down, and it took a lot. We had to invoke the Parliament Act to equalise the age of consent because the House of Lords would just not let it through. The same as well for *Section 28.* Over time we tried to repeal it but the Lords blocked the piece of legislation that it was in.

Archive news clip – police marching at Gay Pride and being told to halt – one of the marching police then kneels and proposes to a man in the crowd.

Lord Cashman: There has been an incredible shift in policing attitudes, a lot to do with changes in the law. We must never forget that the police are there to enforce the law.

Lord Paddick: There is still quite a lot of homophobia in the police service. When senior police officers stood at the front of the room extolling the virtues of diversity, you could tell who really meant it and who were just reading the words off the card.

Lord Cashman: But when it was signalled by politicians that the laws had to change and that it was no longer acceptable, the police moved swiftly. What's incredible is that you see people, LGBT people, marching in their uniforms, policewomen and policemen. These are the people who have changed attitudes.

Baroness Barker: And, in 2002, the then Blair government put forward this change to the Adoption and Children Act. It was really the first recognition that families could come in lots of different shapes and sizes.

Archive news broadcast: "And next tonight there is a campaign under way this week to encourage more gay and lesbian couples to adopt children."

Yotam Ottolenghi: I always knew I wanted children and it's probably in my genes, because the Jewish genes... I mean not having a child is a big deal. Early on I thought it was impossible, and then gradually it became possible and you could see more gay people and lesbians having children. And, in the late 2000s, I realised I'd better start doing it or it was going to be too late.

Dan Gillespie-Sells: My mum, whose name is Kath, and my other mum whose name is Dilis – because my mum was my biological mother we called her mum, and Dilis we called Dilis. And I suppose, because it's an unusual kind of Irish name I assumed that everyone else had a Dilis – for me that was the term – dad, mum, Dilis. So I thought, uncle, aunty, grandmother, I thought that was a family role. So when I went to school I realised that not everyone else had one of those.

Peter Tatchell: 2004 was the real breakthrough for trans people with the passage of the Gender Recognition Act. For the first time, trans people were legally allowed to change their gender on official documents, like passports.

Matthew Todd: I think young people, actually a lot of young people, do care about the whole spectrum of the whole rainbow, and all the different types of people that make up the whole family, especially trans issues. It's been an amazing thing to see transgender people and awareness come out of the shadows.

Lord Smith: We probably, I think, still have rather a lot of ground to make up on the 'T' bit of LGBT.

Archive news clip: Transgender people don't just want to be tolerated, they want to be celebrated. But it's clear public attitudes are changing. A recent Sky poll found that almost half the people in the UK think there is nothing morally wrong with gender reassignment.

Stephanie Hirst: Do you know what it is, it's literally, it's tits or death. It's whether you do it or you die. Because you get to a point where you can't survive.

Jake Graf: I mean for me, I think a trans woman is totally a woman and I think a trans man is totally a man, if that's how he feels and how he defines himself.

Paris Lees: Yeah, I don't need a justification, it's just, this is how I am. I'm not hurting anybody, and if I want to call myself a woman, then I am.

Jake Graf: I think what I'm saying, I guess, there are so many different parts of the spectrum that I don't think anything is a 'real man' or a 'real woman'.

Paris Lees: Trans people have existed in every recorded culture around the world throughout history. The only thing that's changed is the way that other people within those societies have treated us.

Archive news broadcast: Awareness has been steadily growing, not least because of trans women like Tara Hudson, detained in all-male prison, she's now being released, but three others took their own lives.

Manjinder Singh Sidhu: In Hinduism you have hermaphrodite, transgender, lesbians and gays. All these things existed, but it was only when the British colonisers came and brought Section 377 and outlawed it all, did that change.

Shon Faye: All LGBT people, trans people especially, have experienced higher rates of suicide, or attempted suicide, mental health problems, abuse and so there are more gay people.... and poverty, because a lot of places still won't hire you.

Jason Prince: I think mental health is the worst it's ever been on the gay scene.

Matthew Todd: There was a young man that wrote to tell me that every day he'd been homophobically abused. He was known as the local queer, he would be spat at, he would get abuse on the bus, every day that would happen. There was another young man who wrote to tell me that his stepfather wouldn't let him have dinner with his siblings in case he turned them gay.

Jason Prince: I meet people quite often when they are first in London, and I've seen the deterioration.

Stephen K. Amos: I do a lot of work for a charity called the Albert Kennedy Trust, which basically just deals with young, vulnerable teenagers who have been kicked out of their family home.

Jason Prince: A lot of them are on the game, and you know at one time I just couldn't believe there was just like a whole generation of boys that there first option was to go on the game.

Stephen K. Amos: Parents will kick their children out for being gay.

Jason Prince: The stigma is still there, so if a young lad like that catches HIV, even though there is no need for them to be ill, even, or die if they can get it under control, the fact is a lot of them go off the rails.

Matthew Todd: The issue of chemsex parties has gotten a lot of attention over the last couple of years. I think it's because it's been growing probably for the last decade or so. It's just a case of where people, I guess, are going less to bars and clubs and are meeting up via apps like Grindr and Scruff and others to have house parties where people take drugs and have sex. What's not to like?

Commentator in archive news clip: "Five gay men are being diagnosed with HIV every single day in London, just in London. That's a huge number."

Matthew Todd: It's just the fact that these drugs are incredibly powerful and they kill lots of people.

Jason Prince: The next generation of boys coming out, even though they can be open with their straight friends and with their families, I think we've got a different set of problems that haven't been dealt with before in this country.

Commentator in archive news clip: "Milestone after milestone has passed, an equal age of consent, discrimination at work outlawed. Civil marriages introduced."

Archive news clip with Peter Tatchell: "We have moved mountains in that period since the late Sixties to now. Every major legal discrimination bar the ban on same-sex marriage has been repealed. For thousands and thousands of gay people this will be a joyous occasion because it will mean that society finally does recognise our love as equal."

TITLE: 2007 – 40 Years Legal

Archive news report: Same-sex couples in England and Wales who have had the right to enter into a civil partnership since 2005 will now be able to marry.
Archive news report, Tonight At Ten: "Plans to allow gay couples to marry have been approved by MPs."
Prime Minister David Cameron in archive news clip: "Gay people should be able to get married too. This is yes, about equality, but it's also about making our society stronger."

Matt Lucas: We've had to find different pathways to love and affection. We've had to find it where we can, it's been in stolen moments with different people, sometimes more than we want it to be, because the idea, the notion of falling in love with another man has terrified people, straight people, over the years.

Baroness Barker: People have families, make families, are responsible to bring up children who are happy. And always have actually.

Dan Gillespie-Sells: If you have gay parents, it's amazing, it's great, it's like this wonderful thing where you know that whatever you choose is going to be great. But you still don't want to talk about it. This was one of the big issues – it's like, who wants to talk about sex with their parents.

Yotam Ottolenghi: Whether you're a gay or straight man it matters less and less.

Stephanie Hirst: Anybody can be attracted to anybody.

Tom Robinson: My bisexual side came round and smacked me round the back of the head and I found myself very inconveniently in love with a woman.

Yotam Ottolenghi: That fluidity is something which makes so much sense.

Evan Davis: I notice from young people that they just seem to mix everything up much more.

Stephen Fry: It's not just about society accepting gay people, it's about gay people accepting themselves.

Olly Alexander: It's become more common, it's like an emerging kind of consciousness about these identities and sexual fluidity, gender fluidity.

Matthew Parris: Fewer people give a toss about it.

Stephanie Hirst: I think, the 50 years since the decriminalisation act and where we are today – look how far we have come.

Sir Ian McKellen: We got rid of *Section 28*. We made it legal for gay people to serve in the military if they wanted to. We made it legal for gay people to teach. We made it illegal for anyone to be sacked on the grounds of sexuality. We established an equal age of consent, and now it is illegal to discriminate on grounds of sexuality, so how the world has changed. It used to be illegal to talk positively about homosexuality in schools and now it's required by the law, and that's been the revolution. But no, there's still more to be done, and you know four or five years ago, Michael was walking through Trafalgar Square. He'd just got a job. He was a civil servant, he'd been out of work for a long time and he and his husband or gay partner were arms round each other celebrating. The pubs had just shut and as they passed the lions there, three teenagers spied a couple of "queers", "faggots", "bender", "shirt lifter", all those charming expressions. And Michael was feeling pretty chipper and confident and went up to them and said, "Come on, what's the matter? Yes, I'm gay...." At which point the lad kicked him behind his knees and as his head hit the flagstones one of the girls, who had high heels, stamped on his head. And she did it again. Until she'd killed him. In our capital city. Well, she's in prison of course, but where did she learn that? What did she think she was doing? What was it inside her that made her think that she could do that to anybody on the grounds that she didn't like the fact that they were gay? Nobody is born prejudiced, they learn it, and they can unlearn it very, very quickly. We are all members of these minorities, there is no such thing as the majority. It doesn't exist, not in the majority of sameness. Thank God we are all different, and as you look around here you see every single face is different. It's just wonderful isn't it. And if every face is different, every personality is different, every inside is different and, for goodness sake, every sexuality could be different.

TITLE: 2017 – 50 Years Legal

Clip of Tom Robinson singing 'Glad to be Gay' live in concert

END

INDEX

A

B

G

H

T